Lao for Beginners

by
Buasawan Simmala
(ບົວສະຫວັນ ສິມມາລາ)
and
Benjawan Poomsan Becker
(ເບັນຈະວັນ ພູມແສນ ເບັກເກີ)

PAIBOON
PUBLISHING

ພາສາລາວ

Lao for Beginners

Copyright ©2009 by Paiboon Publishing

(ສຳນັກພິມໄພບູນ)

Printed in Thailand

Paiboon Poomsan Publishing
582 Amarinniwate Village 2
Nawamin Road 90, Bungkum
Bangkok 10230
THAILAND
☏ 662-509-8632
Fax 662-519-5437

Paiboon Publishing
PMB 256, 1442A Walnut Street
Berkeley, California USA 94709
☏ 1-510-848-7086, 1-800-837-2979
Fax 1-510-666-8862, 1-866-800-1840
Email: orders@paiboonpublishing.com
www.paiboonpublishing.com

สำนักพิมพ์ไพบูลย์ภูมิแสน
582 หมู่บ้านอัมรินทร์นิเวศน์ 2
ถ. นวมินทร์ 90 เขตบึงกุ่ม
ก.ท.ม. 10230
☏ 662-509-8632
โทรสาร 662-519-5437

Email: orders@paiboonpublishing.com
www.paiboonpublishing.com

Cover and graphic design by Douglas Morton/APMS

Edited by Oun Khamvanhthong and Kamontip Topanya

Voice Talent: Craig Becker, Buasawan Simmala, Johnathon Jamison, Saikham Jamison, Oun Khamvanhthong and Bouaphet Sygnavong

ISBN 9784887521871

Printed by Chulalongkorn University Printing House
Tel. 0-2218-3563, 0-2218-3557
http://www.cuprint.chula.ac.th

Introduction

Lao for Beginners is designed both for people who are just starting to study the Lao language for the first time and for those who want to improve their basic Lao. It teaches all four basic language skills—speaking, listening (when used with the audio CDs), reading and writing. The first part of each lesson teaches vocabulary and sentence structure and includes a vocabulary list with Lao spelling, transliteration and definitions in English.

The transliteration system assists you with pronunciation while you are learning the Lao alphabet. It's important that you learn to properly pronounce the tones and sounds of Lao. Although *Lao for Beginners* is written with self-study in mind, as well as classroom use, a Lao teacher or tutor should listen to and correct your pronunciation, especially at the beginning.

We encourage beginning students of Lao to learn the alphabet. Even though conversation may be your principal goal, the Lao alphabet is almost 100% phonetic and studying it will reinforce speaking and listening skills as well as reading and writing. Wean yourself off of transliteration as soon as possible. You won't regret the extra effort spent learning the Lao writing system.

The second part of each lesson teaches basic reading and writing of the Lao language. It provides a guided step-by-step introduction to the consonants, vowels, tone rules, and other features of the written language.

Written Lao uses no spaces between words. In this text, however, we usually separate the words with a space to help you get started reading the Lao script more quickly.

The appendix features a section with useful words and phrases that you can use as a quick reference to start using some Lao right away with minimal effort.

Characteristics of the Lao language that are different from English include:

* There are no variant or plural forms for adjectives and nouns.

* Adjectives follow the noun.
  In Lao we say "car white" (lot sĭi kǎao)
  instead of "white car."

* There are no verb conjugations in Lao. We understand tenses from the context or from adverbs of time.

* There are no articles (a, an, the).

* There is no verb 'to be' with adjectives.
  "You're beautiful" would be "You beautiful" (jâo ngáam).

* There are ending particles that imply the needs and feelings of the speaker.

* Classifiers are used with virtually all nouns.

* Lao usually omits the subject of a sentence when it is understood from the context.

* Lao is a tonal language.
  If the tone is not correct, you won't be easily understood, even if your pronunciation is otherwise perfect.

* Lao is almost 100% phonetic. There are only a very few words that are pronounced slightly different from the way they are written.

You can use this book in combination with our Lao-English, English-Lao Dictionary for Non-Lao Speakers to expand your vocabulary and language usage.

We hope you enjoy this language course and are certain you will find it fun and worthwhile to communicate with the friendly Lao people in their own language.

Transliteration

Different Lao books and dictionaries use different transliteration systems. Many of them are oriented towards speakers of French and are not as helpful to English speakers. Every attempt was made to keep the transliteration in this book consistent, accurate and simple for English speakers. We use the standard international phonetic alphabet for tones and other sounds not normally represented in written English.

You will find that words are not always pronounced exactly as they are transliterated. In colloquial speech people speak fast, drop sounds and words, change some consonants (e.g. some people change "hoong-hian" to "loong-lian" - school), vowels, vowel length (e.g. "hiin" to "hin" - stone) and tones. Also, there are regional speech differences. We picked the pronunciation that is most widely and commonly used.

Five Tones vs Six Tones

Some linguists have identified six tones in the Lao language and others say there are five. According to the Lao high school textbooks published by the Ministry of Education of Laos, there are six tones in the northern dialect and five tones in the central and southern regions. The people in the north tend to speak more slowly and draw out words.

We use the five tone system in this book. It is the most commonly used and is the one promulgated by the Ministry of Education of Laos in their effort to standardize the Lao language.

Exceptions

Written Lao, especially as now standardized by the Lao government, is very phonetic. Nevertheless, some words are most commonly pronounced differently from the way they should be according to the rules of written Lao. This is especially true of multi-syllabic words in which tones and sounds can get dropped or changed in normal speech. When there is a difference between the way a word is written and the way it is spoken, we transliterate it according to the way it is most commonly spoken. For example, the word "post office" is transliterated as "bpai-sa-nii" instead of "bpai-sa-nii."

Changes in Tones

Even though Lao is tonal and each syllable has its own tone, Lao tends to change tones in many circumstances.

First, the tones of certain words can change according to where they are placed in a sentence. For example: people from the Vientiane area would change a middle consonant word from low tone to rising tone when it is placed at the end of a sentence or when it stands by itself (like when you hear it said on the audio CDs). There is no change in tone when it is placed in the middle of a sentence.

> e.g.　　bpài is changed to bpăi.
> kòi bɔɔ bpăi. = I'm not going.
> kòi bɔɔ bpài dta-làat. = I'm not going to the market.
> dìi is changed to dĭi.
> sa-bàai-dìi bɔɔ. = How are you?
> sa-bàai-dĭi. = I'm well.

Secondly, you may hear different tones for the same word in different regions. People in the north speak more slowly and tend do draw out words. For example the word "many" will sound more like a falling tone "lâai" rather than "lăai" the rising tone. It also sounds longer.

Thirdly, people have different levels of tone or pitch when they speak. This oocurs in all languages but may be more noticeable in Lao. Keep this in mind when you hear individuals pronounce words in a non-standard way.

Finally, Lao has many ending particles. We do not explain the usage of all the particles in this book for beginners. Many ending particles are used to emphasize the needs and feelings of the speaker. They tend to change tones according to the nuances of the speaker's message.

You will hear different voices on our audio. The Lao speakers are from three regions of Laos. The two female voices are from Vientiane, one male speaker is from the north and one from the south.

Lao is a forgiving language when it comes to tones and pronunciation. Fortunately, since there is so much individual and regional variation, people are accustomed to hearing words pronounced in different ways. You will probably be understood in spite of imperfect tones and vowel length— assuming that you are not too far off and don't sound like you are saying something totally different.

Table of Contents

Guide to Pronunciation   9

Lesson 1   17
greetings; yes-no questions; personal pronouns;
cardinal and ordinal numbers; the Lao writing system;
consonant classes; determining tones in written Lao;
middle consonants; long vowels; tone marks

Lesson 2   39
'bpèn' and 'yuu' (to be); more vowels; live and dead
syllables; tone rules for middle consonants

Lesson 3   61
colors; 'jǎ' (future tense); 'dâi' (can); more vowels;
complex vowels; final consonants;
ten vowels that change their forms;
tone rules for middle consonants (cont.)

Lesson 4   87
telling time; high consonants;
tone rules for high consonants

Lesson 5   107
days of the week; months; tone marks with
high consonants; low consonants introduced

8

Lesson 6 125
'ào' (to get), 'yàak' (to want); 'gamlang' (to be ... ing);
tone rules for low consonants

Lesson 7 145
'dâi-yín' (to hear); 'jɯɯ' (to remember);
'nɔ́ɔn-lǎp' (to fall asleep); 'bəng' (to look);
tone rules for low consonants (cont.)

Lesson 8 165
body parts; everyday life; silent ຫ (hɔ̌ɔ)

Lesson 9 179
family and kinship terms; occupations; animals;
punctuation marks; practice reading short sentences

Lesson 10 199
comparisons; adjectives; classifiers; practice reading
short sentences and paragraphs

Appendix I 227
Useful Words and Phrases

Appendix I 247
Summary of the Lao Writing System

Appendix II 255
Test and Writing Exercise Answers

Guide to Pronunciation

Consonants

b	as in baby	bìn - to fly
d	as in doll	dìi - good
f	as in fun	fái - fire
g	as in gold	gìn - eat
h	as in honey	hàa - five
j	as in jet	jĕt - seven
k	as in kiss	kón - person
l	as in love	líng - monkey
m	as in money	míi - to have
n	as in need	náa - rice field
ñ	as in español	ñúng - mosquito ("ny" in other books)
p	as in pretty	pán - thousand
s	as in sex	sii - four
t	as in tender	tŏng - bag
w	as in woman	wíi - fan
y	as in you	yàa - medicine
kw	as in queen	kwúan - smoke
gw	as in Guam	gwaa - more
ng	as in ringing	ngúu - snake
dt	as in stop	dtàa - eye
bp	as in spot	bpài - to go

The /dt/ sound lies between the /d/ and the /t/. Similarly, the /bp/ is between /b/ and /p/ (in linguistic terms, they are both unvoiced and unaspirated). Unlike English, /ng/ frequently occurs at the beginning of words in Lao.

Lao used to have the rolled "r" sound, but it has dropped out of common speech and been replaced by the "l" sound.

The new Lao writing system does not have consonant cluster sounds in either the initial or final position of a syllable. In this book final consonant sounds of a syllable are transliterated as follows:

k is used for ກ.

t is used for ດ.

p is used for ບ.

n is used for ນ.

ng is used for ງ.

m is used for ມ.

əi, əəi are used for ເ◌ັຍ.

aao is used for -າວ.

Vowels

Most Lao vowels have two versions, short and long. Short vowels are clipped and cut off at the end. Long ones are drawn out. This book shows short vowels with a single letter and long vowels with double letters ('a' for short; 'aa' for long).

The 'ʉ' has no comparable sound in English. Try saying 'u' while spreading your lips in as wide a smile as possible. If the sound you are making is similar to one you might have uttered after stepping on something disgusting, you are probably close!

Short & Long Vowels

a	like a in Alaska	mán - it
aa	like a in father	hàa - five
i	like i in tip	sĭp - ten
ii	like ee in see	sii - four
u	like oo in boot	yŭt - stop
uu	like u in ruler	sŭun - zero
ʉ	like u in ruler, but with a smile	nʉng - one
ʉʉ	like ʉ but longer	mʉ́ʉ - hand
e	like e in pet	jĕt - seven
ee	like a in pale	péeng - song
ɛ	like a in cat	lɛ - and
ɛɛ	like a in sad	dɛ̀ɛng - red
ə	like er in teacher without the "r" sound	bəng - to look
əə	like ə but longer	bpə̀ət - open
o	like o in note	pŏm - hair
oo	like o in go	lôok - world
ɔ	like au in caught	gɔ̆ - island
ɔɔ	like aw in law	nɔ́ɔn - to sleep

Complex Vowels

The following dipthongs are combinations of the above vowels.

ai	mai - new	aai	sáai - sand
ao	máo - drunk	aao	kǎao - white
ia	bìa - beer	iao	nǐao - sticky
ua	hǔa - head	uai	lúai - rich
ʉa	hʉ́a - boat	ʉai	mʉai - tired
ɔi	kɔ̀i - I, me	ɔɔi	nɔ́ɔi - little
ooi	dòoi - by	əəi	kə̀əi - ever
ui	kui - flute	iu	hǐu - hungry
eo	leo - to fight	eeo	hěeo - cliff
εo	těo - row	εεo	lɛ̂εo - already

Short and Long Vowels Compared

Short Vowel			Long Vowel		
kǎo	(ເຂົາ)	horn	kǎao	(ຂາວ)	white
jàn	(ຈັນ)	moon	jàan	(ຈານ)	plate
ñáng	(ຍັງ)	yet	ñáang	(ຍາງ)	rubber oil
kún	(ຄຸນ)	gratitude	kúun	(ຄູນ)	to multiply
sǎi	(ໃສ)	clear	sǎai	(ສາຍ)	line
mài	(ໄໝ້)	burn	màai	(ໝ້າຍ)	widower
nái	(ໃນ)	in	náai	(ນາຍ)	master
háo	(ເຮົາ)	we	hǎao	(ຫາວ)	to yawn
jǎk	(ຈັກ)	machine	jàak	(ຈາກ)	from

Tone Marks

Because Lao is a tonal language, its pronunciation presents new challenges for English speakers. If the tone is wrong, you will not be easily understood even if everything else is correct. Lao uses five tones (some books say there are six). For example, to pronounce a rising tone your voice starts at a low pitch and goes up (much like asking a question in English). The phonetic transliteration in this book uses tone marks over the vowels to show the tone for each word. Note that the tone marks used for transliteration are different from those used in Lao script.

Tone Marks (Transliteration)

Tone	Tone Symbol	Example	
mid	None	maa	ໝ່າ
low	`	màa	ໝ້າ
falling	^	mâa	ມ້າ
high	´	máa	ມາ
rising	ˇ	mǎa	ໝາ

Some books use this mark ‿ for the low tone, e.g. maa.

Tones

Have a native speaker pronounce each tone using sample words in the following pages. Listen to it, try to say it and see if you can hear the tones correctly.

Samples of the five tones

Words with **mid** tone:

yuu	(ຢູ່)	to be, to live
bɔɔ	(ບໍ່)	no, not
sii	(ສີ່)	four
gai	(ໄກ່)	chicken
mii	(ໝີ່)	noodle

Words with **low** tone:

hàa	(ຫ້າ)	five
kào	(ເຂົ້າ)	rice, to enter
pàa	(ຜ້າ)	cloth
yàak	(ຢາກ)	to want
kài	(ໄຂ້)	sickness

Words with **falling** tone:

sâai	(ຊ້າຍ)	left
gâi	(ໃກ້)	near
nîi	(ນີ້)	this
sâo	(ເຊົ້າ)	morning
lîn	(ລີ້ນ)	tongue

Words with **high** tone:

kón	(ถิม)	person
láao	(ลาว)	Lao
tái	(ไທ)	Thai
hían	(ธฐม)	to study
náa	(มา)	rice field

Words with **rising** tone:

mǎa	(ໝา)	dog
sǔung	(สูງ)	tall
mǔu	(ໝູ)	pig
kǎao	(຺ຂາວ)	white
sǎam	(สาม)	three

Tones, Short-Long Vowels, Similar Consonants and Vowel Sounds

When you are not understood, often you are saying the tone wrong. However, the length of the vowel is also very important. Try to get the vowel length correct. This will help you to be understood better while you are still learning to master the tones.

Here are some examples of words with different tones and their meanings.

mâa	(ม้า)	horse
máa	(มา)	to come
mǎa	(ໝາ)	dog
mai	(ใໝ່)	new
mài	(ໄໝ້)	to burn
mái	(ໄມ)	mile
mǎi	(ໄໝ)	silk

kaao	(ຂາວ)	news
káao	(ຄາວ)	fishy
kǎao	(ຂາວ)	white

kao	(ເຂົາ)	knee
kào	(ເຂົາ)	to enter, rice
kǎo	(ເຂົາ)	animal horn, he/she

sii	(ສີ)	four
sǐi	(ສີ)	color

sùa	(ເສື້ອ)	shirt
sǔa	(ເສື້ອ)	tiger

hûu	(ຮູ້)	to know
húu	(ຮູ)	hole
hǔu	(ຫູ)	ear

Comparison of Similar Sounds

dìi	(ດີ)	good	dtìi	(ຕີ)	to hit
bài	(ໃບ)	leaf	bpài	(ໄປ)	to go
nǔu	(ຫນູ)	mouse	ngúu	(ງູ)	snake
pět	(ເຜັດ)	spicy	bpět	(ເປັດ)	duck
kɨang	(ເຄື່ອງ)	thing	kɔng	(ເຄິ່ງ)	half
dào	(ເດົາ)	to guess	dtào	(ເຕົາ)	stove
pûun	(ພື້ນ)	floor	bpùun	(ປືນ)	gun

Lesson 1

greetings; yes-no questions; personal pronouns; cardinal and ordinal numbers; the Lao writing system; consonant classes; determining tones in written Lao; middle consonants; long vowels; tone marks

bŏt-tii nɯng   ບົດທີ ນຶ່ງ   Lesson 1

kám-săp   ຄໍາສັບ   Vocabulary

kɔ̀i	ຂ້ອຍ	I, me
jâo/pûak-jâo	ເຈົ້າ / ພວກເຈົ້າ	you/you (plural)
sɯɯ	ຊື່	name
sa-bàai-dìi	ສະບາຍດີ	"Good day."
sa-bàai-dìi/sa-bàai-dìi-bɔɔ		"How are you?"[1]
ສະບາຍດີ/ ສະບາຍດີບໍ່?		
bpen-jang-dǎi	ເປັນຈັ່ງໃດ?	"How is it going?"
sa-bàai-dìi	ສະບາຍດີ	to be fine
ñín-dii-tii-dâi-pop-(gǎp)-jâo		Nice to meet you.
ຍິນດີທີ່ໄດ້ພົບ (ກັບ) ເຈົ້າ		
ñín-dii-tii-dâi-pop-jâo-kɯ́ɯ-gan		Nice to meet you too.
ຍິນດີທີ່ໄດ້ພົບເຈົ້າຄືກັນ		
kɔ̌ɔ-tôot	ຂໍໂທດ	Excuse me.
bɔɔ-bpen-ñǎng	ບໍ່ເປັນຫຍັງ	It doesn't matter.[2]
kɔ̀ɔp-jài	ຂອບໃຈ	Thank you.
la/lɛ̂ɛo/dèe	ລະ/ແລ້ວ/ເດ	"What about .....?"
bpɯ̂m	ປຶ້ມ	book
nǎng-sɯ̌ɯ-pím	ໜັງສືພິມ	newspaper
móong	ໂມງ	watch, clock
bpàak-gàa	ປາກກາ	pen
sɔ̌ɔ-dàm	ສໍດໍາ	pencil
tǒng	ຖົງ	bag
pɛ̌ɛn-tii	ແຜນທີ່	map
bpɯ̂m-kǐan	ປຶ້ມຂຽນ	notebook
nîi	ນີ້	this
nân	ນັ້ນ	that
pûun/pûn	ພຸ້ນ	that (further away)

mɛɛn/mɛn ແມ່ນ	to be (something)[3]
ñăng ຫຍັງ	what
mɛɛn/mɛɛn-lɛ́ɛo ແມ່ນ/ແມ່ນແລ້ວ	yes[4]
bɔɔ ບໍ່	no, not[5]
bɔɔ ບໍ່	a question particle[5]
mɛɛn-bɔɔ ແມ່ນບໍ່	..... right?
lŭu ຫຼື	or
gɔɔ ກໍ່	also
kào-jai bɔɔ ເຂົ້າໃຈບໍ່	Understand?
kào-jai ເຂົ້າໃຈ	(I) understand.
bɔɔ kâo-jai ບໍ່ເຂົ້າໃຈ	(I) don't understand.

1. sa-bàai-dìi can be used in greeting or leave-taking at any
    time of day or night.
2. bɔɔ-bpen-ñăng has the following meanings: it doesn't matter;
    that's all right; not at all; it's nothing; never mind; don't
    mention it; forget it; you're welcome, etc.
3. You may hear this word pronounced either short or long.
4. The more polite way to say "mɛɛn" (ແມ່ນ) is "dòoi" (ໂດຍ).
5. bɔɔ (ບໍ່) is used to form a negative and used as a question particle
    placed at the end of sentences to form yes-no questions.

    e.g.   dìi   = good
                bɔɔ dìi = not good
                dii bɔɔ = Is it good?

Conversation 1

Jampa:	sa-bàai-dìi.
จำปา:	ສະບາຍດີ.
	Hello.
John:	sa-bàai-dìi.
จอม :	ສະບາຍດີ.
	Hello.
Jampa:	kɔ̀i sɯ̀ɯ jàm-bpàa. jâo sɯ̀ɯ nyǎng.
จำปา:	ຂ້ອຍ ຊື່ ຈຳປາ. ເຈົ້າ ຊື່ ຫຍັງ.
	My name is Jampa. What's your name?
John:	kɔ̀i sɯ̀ɯ jɔ̀ɔn. ñín-dìi tii dâi pop gǎp jâo.
จອມ :	ຂ້ອຍ ຊື່ ຈອມ. ຍິນດີ ທີ່ ໄດ້ ພົບ ກັບ ເຈົ້າ.
	My name is John. Nice to meet you.
Jampa:	ñín-dìi kɯ̀ɯ-gan.
จำปา:	ຍິນດີ ຄືກັນ.
	Nice to meet you, too.

Conversation 2

Kamsai:	sa-bàai-dìi bɔɔ.
ຄำใส:	ສະບາຍດີ ບໍ່?
	How are you?
Ginny:	sa-bàai dìi. lɛ̀ɛo jâo děe.
จิมบ̌:	ສະບາຍດີ. ແລ້ວ ເຈົ້າ ເດ?
	I'm fine. How about you?
Kamsai:	kɔ̀i gɔɔ sa-bàai dìi. kɔ̀ɔp-jài.
ຄำใส:	ຂ້ອຍ ກໍ່ ສະບາຍ ດີ. ຂອບໃຈ.
	I'm also fine. Thank you.

bpà-ñòok   · ປະໂຫຍກ   Sentences

1. A: nîi mɛɛn bpûm bɔɔ.
    ນີ້ ແມ່ນ ປຶມ ບໍ?
    Is this a book?

    B: mɛɛn-lɛ́ɛo, nîi mɛɛn bpûm.
    ແມ່ນແລ້ວ, ນີ້ ແມ່ນ ປຶມ.
    Yes, this is a book.

2. A: nân mɛɛn bpûm-kǐan bɔɔ.
    ນັ້ນ ແມ່ນ ປຶມຂຽນ ບໍ?
    Is that a notebook?

    B: bɔɔ, nan bɔɔ mɛɛn bpûm-kǐan.
    ບໍ່, ນັ້ນ ບໍ ແມ່ນ ປຶມຂຽນ.
    No, that is not a notebook.

3. A: nîi mɛɛn ñǎng.
    ນີ້ ແມ່ນ ຫຍັງ?
    What is this?

    B: nân mɛɛn tǒng.
    ນັ້ນ ແມ່ນ ຖົງ.
    That is a bag.

4. A: an-nîi mɛɛn móong lǔu bpàak-gaa.
    ອັນນີ້ ແມ່ນ ໂມງ ຫລື ປາກກາ?
    Is this a watch or a pen?

    B: an-nân bpàak-gaa.
    ອັນນັ້ນ ປາກກາ
    That is a pen.

5. A: kào-jài bɔɔ.
    ເຂົ້າໃຈ ບໍ?
    Do you understand?

    B: kào-jài.
    ເຂົ້າໃຈ
    Yes, (I understand).

    C: bɔɔ, bɔɔ kào-jài.
    ບໍ່, ບໍ ເຂົ້າໃຈ
    No, (I don't understand).

6. A: kɔ̌ɔ-tôot.
    ຂໍໂທດ.
    Excuse me.
    B: bɔɔ bpèn-ñăng.
    ບໍ່   ເປັນຫຍັງ.
    That's all right.
7. A: kɔ̀ɔp-jài.
    ຂອບໃຈ.
    Thank you.
    B: bɔɔ bpèn-ñăng.
    ບໍ່   ເປັນຫຍັງ.
    You're welcome.

Notes: 1. A lot of Lao people greet each other with bpèn-jang-dăi ເປັນຈັ່ງໃດ.
            ("How is it going?") instead of using sa-bàai-dìi bɔɔ.
        2. The subject of a sentence is often omitted when understood from
            the context.
            e.g. A: jâo sa-bàai-dii bɔɔ. = sa-bàai-dii bɔɔ. (How are you?)
                  B: kɔ̀i sa-bàai-dii. = sa-bàai-dii. (I'm fine.)
        3. Lao has no direct "yes" or "no." We simply repeat the main verb or
            adjective used in the question.
            e.g. A: kào-jài bɔɔ. (Understand?)
                  B: kào-jài. (Understand.)
                  C: bɔɔ kào-jai. (Not understand.)
            Be careful not to use "mɛɛn" for "yes" and "bɔɔ mɛɛn" for "no"
            all the time. Use them primarily when the question is "mɛɛn bɔɔ."

jàm-núan จำนวน **Numbers**

0	sǔun	ສູນ
1	nɯng	ນຶ່ງ
2	sɔ̌ɔng	ສອງ
3	sǎam	ສາມ
4	sii	ສີ່
5	hàa	ຫ້າ
6	hǒk	ຫົກ
7	jĕt	ເຈັດ
8	bpɛ̀ɛt	ແປດ
9	gâo	ເກົ້າ
10	sǐp	ສິບ
11	sǐp-ĕt	ສິບເອັດ
12	sǐp-sɔ̌ɔng	ສິບສອງ
13	sǐp-sǎam	ສິບສາມ
20	sáao	ຊາວ
21	sáao-ĕt	ຊາວເອັດ
22	sáao-sɔ̌ɔng	ຊາວສອງ
30	sǎam-sǐp	ສາມສິບ
31	sǎam-sǐp-ĕt	ສາມສິບເອັດ
32	sǎam-sǐp-sɔ̌ɔng	ສາມສິບສອງ
40	sii-sìp	ສີ່ສິບ
50	hàa-sǐp	ຫ້າສິບ
60	hǒk-sǐp	ຫົກສິບ
70	jĕt-sǐp	ເຈັດສິບ
80	bpɛ̀ɛt-sǐp	ແປດສິບ
90	gâo-sǐp	ເກົ້າສິບ
100	(nɯng) hɔ̂ɔi	ນຶ່ງຮ້ອຍ*
200	sɔ̌ɔng-hɔ̂ɔi	ສອງຮ້ອຍ

300	săam-hɔ̌ɔi	ສາມຮ້ອຍ
1,000	(nɯng) pán	(ນຶ່ງ) ພັນ
2,000	sɔ̌ɔng-pán	ສອງພັນ
3,000	săam-pán	ສາມພັນ
10,000	(nɯng) mɯɯn/sǐp-pán	(ນຶ່ງ) ໝື່ນ/ສິບພັນ
100,000	(nɯng) sɛ̌ɛn/hɔ̌ɔi-pán	(ນຶ່ງ) ແສນ/ຮ້ອຍພັນ
1,000,000	(nɯng) lâan	(ນຶ່ງ) ລ້ານ
10,000,000	sǐp lâan	ສິບລ້ານ
100,000,000	(nɯng) hɔ̌ɔi lâan	(ນຶ່ງ) ຮ້ອຍລ້ານ
1,000,000,000	(nɯng) pán lâan/dtɯ̂ɯ	(ນຶ່ງ) ພັນລ້ານ/ຕື້
10,000,000,000	(nɯng) mɯɯn lâan/sǐp-dtɯ̂ɯ	
		(ນຶ່ງ) ໝື່ນລ້ານ/ສິບຕື້
100,000,000,000	(nɯng) sɛ̌ɛn lâan/hɔ̌ɔi-dtɯ̂ɯ	
		(ນຶ່ງ) ແສນລ້ານ/ຮ້ອຍຕື້
1,000,000,000,000	(nɯng) lâan lâan/gòot	(ນຶ່ງ) ລ້ານລ້ານ/ໂກດ

1.3	nɯng jǔt săam	ນຶ່ງຈຸດສາມ
2 3/5	sɔ̌ɔng gǎp săam suan hàa	ສອງກັບສາມສ່ວນຫ້າ
7^2	jět gàm-láng sɔ̌ɔng	ເຈັດກຳລັງສອງ

* "hɔ̌ɔi" is sometimes pronounced "lɔ̌ɔi."

Notes: For ordinal numbers, add tîi (ທີ່) in front of cardinal numbers.

> e.g.   tîi nɯng (ທີ່ນຶ່ງ) = the first
> tîi sɔ̌ɔng (ທີ່ສອງ) = the second
> tîi săam (ທີ່ສາມ) = the third
> tîi sǐp (ທີ່ສິບ) = the tenth

Test 1

Match the English words with the Lao words.

_____ 1.	watch	a. ñăng ຫນັງ
_____ 2.	book	b. bpàak-gàa ປາກກາ
_____ 3.	pen	c. nîi ນີ້
_____ 4.	this	d. kɔ̀i ຂ້ອຍ
_____ 5.	I	e. móong ໂມງ
_____ 6.	also	f. nân ນັ້ນ
_____ 7.	map	g. kɔ̀i ຂ້ອຍ
_____ 8.	name	h. sɰɰ ຊື້
_____ 9.	what	i. tŏng ຖົງ
_____ 10.	bag	j. bpɰ̂m ປຶ້ມ
		k. pɛ́ɛn-tii ແຜນທີ່
		l. gɔɔ ກໍ

Translate the following into English.

1. jâo sa-bàai dìi bɔɔ.   ເຈົ້າ ສະບາຍດີ ບໍ່?

   _____

2. kâo-jài bɔɔ.   ເຂົ້າໃຈບໍ່?

   _____

3. nîi mɛɛn năng-sɰɰ-pím mɛɛn bɔɔ.   ນີ້ ແມ່ນ ຫນັງສືພິມ ແມ່ນ ບໍ່?

   _____

4. jâo sɰɰ ñăng.   ເຈົ້າ ຊື້ ຫນັງ?

   _____

5. an-nîi mɛɛn pɛ́ɛn-tii lɰɰ sɔ̌ɔ-dam.   ອັນນີ້ ແມ່ນ ແຜນທີ່ ຫລື ສໍດຳ?

   _____

The Lao Writing System

Lao uses an alphabet of 26 consonants, 28 vowels, four tone marks (only two commonly used) and various other symbols for punctuation, numbers, etc. Although there are irregular pronunciations, Lao is generally phonetic. It is pronounced the way it is written. It is even more phonetic than Thai, its relative.

Learning to read and write Lao from the beginning has many advantages. Due to the fact that it is phonetic, you will be reinforcing your listening and speaking skills while learning to read and write. In fact, most people find that their pronunciation is more accurate when reading Lao script. Unlike many transliteration systems, it incorporates all the elements of pronunciation— including tones and vowel length.

The longer you rely on transliteration, the more time you waste reinforcing a writing system that will be virtually useless in Laos. Furthermore, transliteration is confusing with almost as many systems as there are books about Lao. Put a little extra effort into learning the alphabet now! Then you can use Lao script while studying conversation, reinforcing reading and writing skills that will be invaluable to you in Laos.

Consonant Classes

Lao consonants are divided into three classes— high, middle and low. Since it is one of the critical factors in determining a syllable's tone, you must know the consonant class in order to correctly pronounce what you have read.

The names (high, middle and low) of the consonant classes are completely arbitrary. For example, a low consonant may generate a high tone and a high consonant can generate a low tone, etc.

What Determines the Tone

1.   Consonant class: whether the initial consonant is high, middle or low.

2.   Vowel length: whether short or long.

3.   Tone Mark: whether or not there is a tone mark placed above the initial consonant of a syllable. (If the consonant has a superscript vowel, the tone mark is placed above that vowel.)

4.   Final consonant: whether sonorant final or stop final.

Middle Consonants

ອັກສອນກາງ (ăk-sɔ̌ɔn-gàang)

There are eight "middle" consonants in Lao as follows:

Consonant		Consonant Name	Sound
ກ	ກ ໄກ່	gɔ̌ɔ gai - chicken	/g/
ຈ	ຈ ຈອກ	jɔ̌ɔ jɔ̀ɔk - cup, glass	/j/
ດ	ດ ເດັກ	dɔ̌ɔ dĕk - child	/d/
ຕ	ຕ ຕາ	dtɔ̌ɔ dtàa - eye	/dt/
ບ	ບ ແບ້	bɔ̌ɔ bɛ̂ɛ - goat	/b/
ປ	ປ ປາ	bpɔ̌ɔ bpàa - fish	/bp/
ຢ	ຢ ຢາ	yɔ̌ɔ yàa - medicine	/y/
ອ	ອ ໂອ	ɔ̌ɔ òo - bowl	/silent/

Practice Writing the Middle Consonants

All the middle consonants are written with one stroke starting near the **❶**. Notice that you always start with the small circle
where there is one.

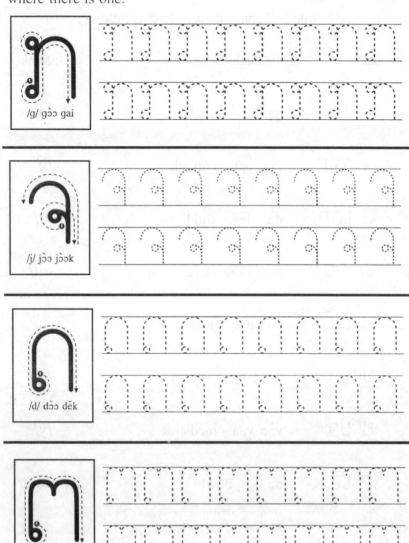

/g/ gɔ̀ɔ gai

/j/ jɔɔ jɔ̀ɔk

/d/ dɔɔ dĕk

/dt/ dtɔɔ dtàa

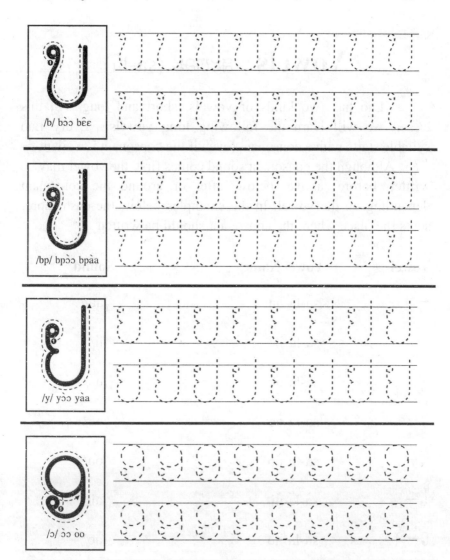

/b/ bɔɔ bɛ̂ɛ

/bp/ bpɔɔ bpàa

/y/ yɔɔ yàa

oo cɔ́ ɔ̀o /ɔ/

Vowels   ສະຫລະ (sà-lǎ)

Lao has two kinds of vowels: short and long. In this lesson we will learn the following **long vowels**. Every Lao syllable starts with a consonant (even if the consonant is a silent ອ /-/). Although the consonant sound comes first, the vowel may be written before, above, below, after or around the consonant depending on the vowel. In the examples below, the dash represents the place where the consonant should be written.

Vowel	Vowel Name	Sound
−ๅ	sà-lǎ àa	/aa/
−ິ	sà-lǎ ìi	/ii/
−ູ	sà-lǎ ùu	/uu/
ເ−	sà-lǎ èe	/ee/
ໂ−	sà-lǎ òo	/oo/
ໃ−	sà-lǎ ài	/ai/
ເ−ົๅ	sà-lǎ ào	/ao/

Practice Writing the Following Vowels

Use ອ /-/ as the consonant when practicing the following vowels. Always start with the small circle where there is one.

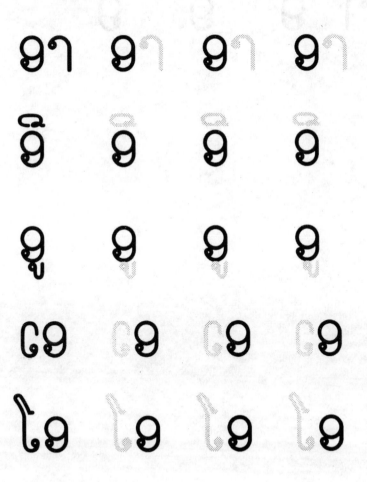

ໄຍ   ໄຍ   ໄຍ   ໄຍ

ເຍົາ   ເຍົາ   ເຍົາ   ເຍົາ

Read the Following Aloud

1. ກາ   ກິ   ກຸ   ເກ   ໂກ   ໄກ   ເກົາ
2. ຈາ   ຈິ   ຈຸ   ເຈ   ໂຈ   ໄຈ   ເຈົາ
3. ຄາ   ຄິ   ຄຸ   ເຄ   ໂຄ   ໄຄ   ເຄົາ
4. ຕາ   ຕິ   ຕຸ   ເຕ   ໂຕ   ໄຕ   ເຕົາ
5. ບາ   ບິ   ບຸ   ເບ   ໂບ   ໄບ   ເບົາ
6. ປາ   ປິ   ປຸ   ເປ   ໂປ   ໄປ   ເປົາ
7. ອາ   ອິ   ອຸ   ເອ   ໂອ   ໄອ   ເອົາ

Tone Marks (Lao Script)

Lao has four tone marks. (The first two are more commonly used.) When a tone mark is used, it is always placed above the initial consonant of the syllable. If the consonant has a superscript vowel, the tone mark is placed above that vowel.

Tone Mark   Name

ˋ
—   mâi èek   (ໄມ້ເອກ)

ˇ
—   mâi tóo   (ໄມ້ໂທ)

ˀ
—   mâi dùi   (ໄມ້ຕີ)

+
—   mâi jăt-dta-wáa (ໄມ້ຈັດຕະວາ)

Tone Marks With Middle Consonants

With middle consonant syllables, all five tones are possible
and all four tone marks can be used. The high and rising tones are
not seen very often.

Tone Mark	Tone Name	Tone	Examples
—	sǐang sǎa-mán	mid	ᨠᩣ (gaa)
None	sǐang èek	low	ᨣᩣ (gàa)
—	sǐang too	falling	ᨣᩣ (gâa)
—	sǐang dtìi	high	ᨣᩣ (gáa)
—	sǐang jǎt-dta-wáa	rising	ᨣᩣ (gǎa)

Read The Following Aloud

1.   ᨠᩣ   ᨣᩣ   ᨣᩣ
2.   ᨤ�5   ᨤ�5   ᨤ�5
3.   ᨦᩩ   ᨦᩩ   ᨦᩩ
4.   ᨣ��   ᨣ�   ᨣ�
5.   ᨵ�2   ᨵ᩠   ᨵ�

6. ໄກ່   ໄກ   ໄກ້

7. ເກົາ   ເກົາ   ເກົາ

8. ຈີ່   ຈີ   ຈີ້

9. ຈຸ່   ຈຸ   ຈຸ້

10. ເຈ່   ເຈ   ເຈ້

11. ໄຈ່   ໄຈ   ໄຈ້

12. ໄຈ່   ໄຈ   ໄຈ້

13. ເຈົາ   ເຈົາ   ເຈົາ

14. ຄຸ່   ຄຸ   ຄຸ້

15. ເຄ່   ເຄ   ເຄ້

16. ໄຄ່   ໄຄ   ໄຄ້

17. ໄຄ່   ໄຄ   ໄຄ້

18. ຄາ່   ຄາ   ຄາ້

19. ເຕ່   ເຕ   ເຕ້

20. ໄຕ່   ໄຕ   ໄຕ້

21. ໄຕ່   ໄຕ   ໄຕ້

22. ເຕົາ   ເຕົາ   ເຕົາ

23. ໄບ່   ໄບ   ໄບ້

24. ໄບ່   ໄບ   ໄບ້

25. ໄບ່   ໄບ   ໄບ້

26. ເບົາ   ເບົາ   ເບົາ

Writing Exercise 1

Transcribe the following into Lao script.

1. dàa _____   11. jài _____

2. gŏo _____   12. dtao _____

3. bâi _____   13. òo _____

4. dtuu _____   14. bpài _____

5. ào _____   15. gûu _____

6. bpŏo_____   16. bŏo _____

7. gao _____   17. jăa _____

8. jîi _____   18. dào _____

9. âi _____   19. gii _____

10. bêe _____   20. âa _____

Lesson 2

'bpèn' and 'yuu' (to be); more vowels; live and dead
syllables; tone rules for middle consonants

bŏt-tii sɔ̌ɔng   ບົດທີ ສອງ   Lesson 2

kám-sǎp   ຄຳສັບ   Vocabulary

tóo-la-sǎp	ໂທລະສັບ	telephone
tóo-la-tat	ໂທລະທັດ	television
wɛn-dtàa	ແຫວ່ນຕາ	eye-glasses
ngə́n	ເງິນ	money
wat-ja-náa-nu-gòm		dictionary
ວັດຈະນານຸກົມ		
hûup/hûup-pâap	ຮູບ/ ຮູບພາບ	picture
jîa	ເຈັ້ຍ	paper
dto	ໂຕະ	table
gâo-îi	ເກົ້າອີ້	chair
hɔ̀ng	ຫ້ອງ	room
hɔ̀ng-nɔ́ɔn	ຫ້ອງນອນ	bedroom
hɔ̂ng-nâm/hɔ̂ng-nâam	ຫ້ອງນ້ຳ	bathroom
hɯ́an	ເຮືອນ	house
bpèn	ເປັນ	to be something
yuu	ຢູ່	to be somewhere (live, stay)
ào	ເອົາ	to get, take
nái	ໃນ	in
tə́ng	ເທິງ	on
dtâi/lum	ໃຕ້/ລຸ່ມ	under
la-waang/waang-gàang		between
ລະວ່າງ/ຫວ່າງກາງ		
gǎp	ກັບ	and, with
bɔɔ dâi	ບໍ່ໄດ້	not
mɯ́ang	ເມືອງ	town, city

kón	ຄົນ	person
kón láao	ຄົນລາວ	Laotian
kón tái	ຄົນໄທ	Thai
kón jìin	ຄົນຈີນ	Chinese
kón ñii-bpun	ຄົນຍີ່ປຸ່ນ	Japanese
kón àa-mée-li-gàa	ຄົນອາເມລິກາ	American[1]
kón fa-lang	ຄົນຝຣັ່ງ	Frenchman[1]
kón gào-lǐi	ຄົນເກົາຫລີ	Korean
kón àng-gǐt	ຄົນອັງກິດ	Englishman
kón-kǎai-kʉang	ຄົນຂາຍເຄື່ອງ	vendor
bpa-têet	ປະເທດ	country
bpa-têet láao/mʉang-láao		Laos
ປະເທດລາວ/ ເມືອງລາວ		
bpa-têet tái/mʉang-tái		Thailand
ປະເທດໄທ/ ເມືອງໄທ		
bpa-têet jìin	ປະເທດຈີນ	China
bpa-têet ñii-bpun	ປະເທດຍີ່ປຸ່ນ	Japan
bpa-têet àa-mée-li-gàa		America
ປະເທດອາເມລິກາ		
bpa-têet àng-gǐt	ປະເທດອັງກິດ	England
páa-sǎa	ພາສາ	language
páa-sǎa láao	ພາສາລາວ	Lao language
páa-sǎa àng-gǐt	ພາສາອັງກິດ	English language
tii	ທີ່	at
yuu-nìi	ຢູ່ນີ້	(over) here
yuu-hàn	ຢູ່ຫັ້ນ	(over) there
yuu-pûn	ຢູ່ພຸ້ນ	(over) there (further)
yuu-sǎi	ຢູ່ໃສ	where
táang	ທາງ	way
sâai	ຊ້າຍ	left

kwŭa/kwăa ຂວາ	right
àn-nîi ອັນນີ້	this one
àn-nân ອັນນັ້ນ	that one
àn-(nân)-pûn ອັນ (ນັ້ນ) ພຸ້ນ	that one (further away)
àn-dăi ອັນໃດ	which one
tao-dăi ເທົ່າໃດ	how much[2]
jăk ຈັກ	how many[2]
gìip ກີບ	kip
dɔ̀n/dɔ̀n-láa ດອນ/ ດອນລາ	dollar
yèn ເຢັນ	yen
tὶὶk ຖືກ	cheap
péɛng ແພງ	expensive
ñâak ຍາກ	difficult
ngaai ງ່າຍ	easy
lăai ຫລາຍ	very, many
háo/pûak háo ເຮົາ/ ພວກເຮົາ	we, us
láao/pən ລາວ/ ເພິ່ນ	he, she, him, her[3]
kăo-jâo/pûak-kăo ເຂົາເຈົ້າ/ ພວກເຂົາ	they, them
mán ມັນ	it

1. You may see different spellings of these words.

2. You use tao-dăi (ເທົ່າໃດ), which means "how much," without a classifier when asking about the quantity of uncountable nouns. But jăk (ຈັກ) which means "how many" must be followed by a classifier.

   e.g. 1. àn-nîi tao-dăi. = How much is this one?

   2. àn-nîi jăk gìip. = How many kip is this one?

   tâo-dăi (ເທົ່າໃດ) is often pronounced tɔɔ-dăi (ທໍໃດ).

3. láao (he, she) is written the same as the word láao (Laotian). pən is used to refer to someone who is older or who the speaker has respect for.

Conversation 1

Bua: kɔ̀i bpèn kón láao. jâo bpèn kón ñǎng.
ບົວ: ຂ້ອຍ ເປັນ ຄົນ ລາວ. ເຈົ້າ ເປັນ ຄົນ ຫຍັງ?
    I'm Lao. What nationality are you?

Tony: kɔ̀i bpèn kón àa-mée-li-gàn.
ໂທນີ: ຂ້ອຍ ເປັນ ຄົນ   ອາເມລິກັນ.

    I'm American.

Bua: jâo yuu sǎi.
ບົວ: ເຈົ້າ ຢູ່ ໃສ?

    Where do you live?

Tony: kɔ̀i yuu sɛɛn-di-ee-gôo.
ໂທນີ: ຂ້ອຍ ຢູ່   ແຊນດິເອໂກ້.

    I live in San Diego.

    jâo děe.
    ເຈົ້າ ເດ?

    And you?

Bua: kɔ̀i yuu wíang-jàn.
ບົວ: ຂ້ອຍ ຢູ່   ວຽງຈັນ.

    I live in Vientiane.

Conversation 2

Jim:	àn-nîi tao-dǎi.
ຈິມ:	ອັນນີ້ ເທົ່າໃດ?

How much is this one?

Konkǎai:	sii-sǐp pán gìip.
ຄົນຂາຍ:	ສີ່ສິບ ພັນ ກີບ.

Forty thousand kip.

Jim:	ôo, pɛ́ɛng pôot.
ຈິມ:	ໂອ, ແພງ ໂພດ.

Oh, that's too expensive.

àn-nân dêe jǎk gìip.

ອັນນັ້ນ ເດ ຈັກ ກີບ?

How much is that one?

Konkǎai:	sǎam-sǐp pán gìip.
ຄົນຂາຍ:	ສາມສິບ ພັນ ກີບ.

Thirty thousand kip.

Jim:	bɔɔ pɛ́ɛng bpàan-dǎi. kɔ̀i ào àn-nîi lǎ.*
ຈິມ:	ບໍ່ ແພງ ປານໃດ. ຂ້ອຍ ເອົາ ອັນນີ້ ລະ.

That's not so expensive. I take this one.

Konkǎai:	kɔ̀ɔp-jài lǎai-lǎai.
ຄົນຂາຍ:	ຂອບໃຈ ຫລາຍໆ.

Thank you very much.

Jim:	bɔɔ bpèn ñǎng.
ຈິມ:	ບໍ່ ເປັນ ຫຍັງ.

You're welcome.

*An ending particle used for emphasis.

bpà-ñòok   ปะໄທຍກ   Sentences

1.   A: tóo-la-săp yuu săi.
        ໄທລະສັບ   ຢູ່ ໃສ?
        Where is the phone?

     B: tóo-la-săp yuu tǎng dto.
        ໄທລະສັບ   ຢູ່ ເທິງ ໂຕະ.
        The phone is on the table.

     C: jâo yuu săi.
        ເຈົ້າ ຢູ່ ໃສ?
        Where are you?

     D: kɔ̀i yuu hǔan.
        ຂ້ອຍ ຢູ່ ເຮືອນ.
        I'm at home.

     E: láao yuu săi.
        ລາວ ຢູ່ ໃສ?
        Where is he?

     F: láao yuu nìi.
        ລາວ ຢູ່ ນີ້.
        He is here.

     G: hɔ̀ng-nâm yuu săi.
        ຫ້ອງນ້ຳ   ຢູ່ ໃສ?
        Where is the bathroom?

     H: hɔ̀ng-nâm yuu táang sâai.
        ຫ້ອງນ້ຳ   ຢູ່ ທາງ ຊ້າຍ.
        The bathroom is on the left.

2.   A: jâo bpèn kón ñǎng.
        ເຈົ້າ ເປັນ   ຄົນ ຫຍັງ?
        What nationality are you?

     B: kɔ̀i bpèn kón àa-mée-li-gàa.
        ຂ້ອຍ ເປັນ   ຄົນ ອາເມລິກາ.
        I am American.

     C: pən bpèn kón ñǎng.
        ເພິ່ນ ເປັນ   ຄົນ ຫຍັງ?
        What nationality is he?

D: pən bpèn kón láao.

ເພິ່ນ ເປັນ ຄົນ ລາວ.

He is Lao.

E: taan táa-náa-gǎ bpèn kón ñǎng.

ທ່ານ ທານາກະ ເປັນ ຄົນ ຫຍັງ?

What nationality is Mr. Tanaka?

F: pən bpèn kón ñii-bpun.

ເພິ່ນ ເປັນ ຄົນ ຍິ່ປຸ່ນ.

He is Japanese.

3. A: àn-nîi tao-dǎi.

ອັນ ນີ້ ເທົ່າໃດ?

How much is this one?

B: àn-nîi hàa-sǐp-pán gìip.

ອັນນີ້ ຫ້າສິບພັນ ກີບ.

This one is 50,0000 kip.

C: àn-nân tao-dǎi.

ອັນ ນັ້ນ ເທົ່າໃດ?

How much is that one?

D: 2,000 yeen.

2,000 ເຢັນ

2,000 yen.

E: àn-nân tao-dǎi.

ອັນນັ້ນ ເທົ່າໃດ?

How much is that?

F: àn-nîi 6 dòn (lâa).

ອັນນີ້ 6 ດອນ (ລ່າ)

This is 6 dollars.

4. A: tóo-la-sǎp yuu tǒng dto mɛɛn bɔɔ.

ໂທລະສັບ ຢູ່ ເທິງ ໂຕະ ແມ່ນ ບໍ່?

Is the phone on the table?

B: mɛɛn-lɛ̂ɛo, tóo-la-sǎp yuu tǒng dtó.

ແມ່ນແລ້ວ, ໂທລະສັບ ຢູ່ ເທິງ ໂຕະ.

Yes, the phone is on the table.

C: bɔɔ, tóo-la-sǎp bɔɔ dâi yuu tǒng dto.

ບໍ່, ໂທລະສັບ ບໍ່ ໄດ້ ຢູ່ ເທິງ ໂຕະ.

No, the phone is not on the table.

5. A: kǎo-jâo bpèn kón ñii-bpun lɯ̌ɯ kón gào-lǐi.
       ເຂົາເຈົ້າ ເປັນ ຄົນ ຍີ່ປຸ່ນ ຫລື ຄົນ ເກົາຫລີ.
       Are they Japanese or Korean?
    B: kǎo-jâo bpèn kón gào-lǐi.
       ເຂົາເຈົ້າ ເປັນ ຄົນ ເກົາຫລີ?
       They are Korean.
6. A: jâo bpèn kón laao mɛɛn bɔɔ.
       ເຈົ້າ ເປັນ ຄົນ ລາວ ແມ່ນ ບໍ່?
       Are you Lao?
    B: mɛɛn, kɔ̀i bpèn kón láao.
       ແມ່ນ, ຂ້ອຍ ເປັນ ຄົນ ລາວ.
       Yes, I'm Lao.
    C: bɔɔ mɛɛn, kɔ̀i bpèn kón tái.
       ບໍ່ ແມ່ນ, ຂ້ອຍ ເປັນ ຄົນ ໄທ.
       No, I'm Thai.
7. A: páa-sǎa láao ñâak bɔɔ.
       ພາສາ ລາວ ຍາກ ບໍ່?
       Is Lao difficult?
    B: ñâak.
       ຍາກ
       Yes. (Difficult)
    C: bɔɔ ñâak.
       ບໍ່ ຍາກ.
       No. (Not difficult)
8. A: páa-sǎa láao ngaai.
       ພາສາ ລາວ ງ່າຍ.
       Lao is easy.
    B: páa-sǎa láao bɔɔ ngaai.
       ພາສາ ລາວ ບໍ່ ງ່າຍ.
       Lao is not easy.
    C: páa-sǎa àng-gǐt ñâak.
       ພາສາ ອັງກິດ ຍາກ.
       English is difficult.
    D: páa-sǎa àng-gǐt bɔɔ ñâak.
       ພາສາ ອັງກິດ ບໍ່ ຍາກ.
       English is not difficult.

9. A: àn-nîi péɛng.

ອັນ ນີ້ ແພງ.

This one is expensive.

B: àn-nîi bɔɔ péɛng.

ອັນ ນີ້ ບໍ່ ແພງ.

This one is not expensive.

10.   bpûm yuu waang-gàang dto găp gâo-îi.

ປຶ້ມ ຢູ່ ທ່າງກາງ ໂຕະ ກັບ ເກົ້າອີ້.

The book is between the table and the chair.

Notes: 1. 'taan' means "you", and it is placed in front of men's first
            names or last names to address them in a polite way.
            For women, it is 'ñáa náang' ບານາງ.

        2. 'bɔɔ dâi' is a negative form like 'not' in English, and is
            used with verbs. It also means 'cannot' (see lesson 3) and
            'did not' (see lesson 7).
            e.g. bpûm bɔɔ dâi yuu tóng dto. = bpûm bɔɔ yuu təng dto.
            (The book is not on the table.)

        3. bɔɔ mɛɛn is a negative form like 'no' or 'not,' and is
            used with nouns.
            e.g. kɔi bɔɔ mɛɛn kón ñii-bpun. (I'm not Japanese.)

        4. There is no exact 'yes' or 'no' in Lao. To answer 'yes,' simply
            repeat the verb or the adjective used in the question. To
            answer 'no,' put bɔɔ before the appropriate word
            (see sentence number 7).

Test 2

Match the English words with the Lao words.

_____ 1. chair   a. tóo-la-sǎp ໂທລະສັບ

_____ 2. table   b. dtâi ໃຕ້

_____ 3. money   c. sɔ̌ɔ-dàm ສໍດຳ

_____ 4. Lao people   d. pən ເພິ່ນ

_____ 5. Japanese   e. kón ang-gǐt ຄົນອັງກິດ

_____ 6. Englishman   f. pέεng ແພງ

_____ 7. in   g. tə́ng ເທິງ

_____ 8. on   h. ñâak ຍາກ

_____ 9. under   i. múang ເມືອງ

_____ 10. telephone   j. hɔ̀ng-nɔ́ɔn ຫ້ອງນອນ

_____ 11. bedroom   k. dto ໂຕະ

_____ 12. television   l. kón láao ຄົນລາວ

_____ 13. he/she   m. gâo-îi ເກົ້າອີ້

_____ 14. expensive   n. ngə́n ເງິນ

_____ 15. difficult   o. kón ñii-bpun ຄົນຍີ່ປຸ່ນ

                                 p. nái ໃນ

                                 q. tóo-la-tat ໂທລະທັດ

                                 r. tùuk ຖືກ

Translate the following into English.

1. tóo-la-sǎp yuu táng gâo-îi.
   ໂທຣະສັບ ຢູ່ ເທິງ ເກົ້າອີ້.

_____

2. láao bpèn kón jìin, bɔɔ mɛɛn kón ñii-bpun.
   ລາວ ເປັນ ຄົນ ຈີນ, ບໍ່ ແມ່ນ ຄົນ ຍີ່ປຸ່ນ.

_____

3. àn-nǐi tao-dǎi.
   ອັນ ນີ້ ເທົ່າໃດ?

_____

4. hɔ̀ng-nâm yuu sǎi.
   ຫ້ອງນ້ຳ ຢູ່ ໃສ?

_____

5. páa-sǎa àng-gìt ñâak lǎai.
   ພາສາ ອັງກິດ ຍາກ ຫລາຍ.

_____

More Vowels

The vowels below include those from lesson one plus five more. Each has a corresponding short vowel form. The difference between a short and long vowel is an important one— it can change a word's meaning by itself. Also, the tone rules for short and long vowels are different.

Short Vowel		Long Vowel	
1. $-$ ៎	/ă/	$-$ ។	/àa/
2. $-$ ៎	/ĭ/	$-$ ៓	/ĭi/
3. $-$ ៎	/ŭ/	$-$ ៓	/ŭu/
4. $-$ ៓	/ŭ/	$-$ ៝	/ùu/
5. ເ$-$ ៎	/ĕ/	ເ$-$	/èe/
6. ແ$-$ ៎	/ɛ̆/	ແ$-$	/ɛ̀ɛ/
7. ໂ$-$ ៎	/ŏ/	ໂ$-$	/òo/
8. ເ$-$ ។ ៎	/ɔ̆/	$-$ ៎	/ɔ̀ɔ/

9. ເ◌ື /ˇə/   ເ◌ື /əə/

10. ◌ົວະ /ˇua/   ◌ົວ /ùa/

11. ເ◌ຍ /ˇia/   ເ◌ຍ /ìa/

12. ເ◌ຶອ /ˇɨa/   ເ◌ຶອ /ɨ̀a/

Practice Writing the Following Vowels

Use /-/ as the consonant when practicing the following vowels.

ອະ   ອະ   ອະ   ອະ

ໍອ   ອ   ອ   ອ

ອ   ອ   ອ   ອ

ဥ္ဂ   ဥ္ဂ   ဥ္ဂ   ဥ္ဂ

ဥ္ဂ   ဥ္ဂ   ဥ္ဂ   ဥ္ဂ

ဗ္ဂေး   ဗ္ဂေ   ဗ္ဂေ   ဗ္ဂေ

ဗ္ဂေး   ဗ္ဂေ   ဗ္ဂေ

ဗ္ဂေ   ဗ္ဂေ   ဗ္ဂေ   ဗ္ဂေ

ဗ္ဂြေး   ဗ္ဂြေ   ဗ္ဂြေ

ဗ္ဂော်း   ဗ္ဂော်း   ဗ္ဂော်း

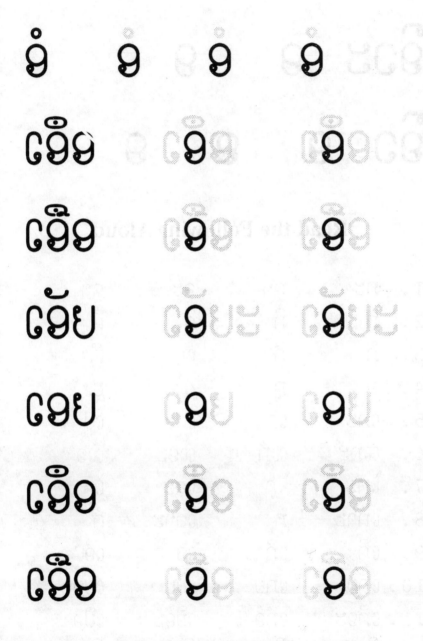

ອີ້ວະ   ອີ້ວະ   ອີ້ວະ

ອີ້ວ   ອີ້ວ   ອີ້ວ   ອີ້ວ

Read the Following Aloud

1. ກະ   ກາ   ຈະ   ຈາ
2. ກິ   ກີ   ຄິ   ຄີ
3. ກຶ   ກື   ຄຶ   ຄື
4. ກຸ   ກູ   ປຸ   ປູ
5. ເກະ   ເກ   ເປະ   ເປ
6. ແກະ   ແກ   ແອະ   ແອ
7. ໂກະ   ໂກ   ໂຈະ   ໂຈ
8. ເກາະ   ກໍ   ເຄາະ   ຄໍ
9. ເກິ   ເກື   ເຊິ   ເຊື
10. ເກຍ   ເກຍ   ເບຍ   ເບຍ
11. ເກືອະ   ເກືອ   ເປືອະ   ເປືອ
12. ກິວະ   ກິວ   ຄິວະ   ຄິວ

Live and Dead Syllables
(ຄຳເປັນ–ຄຳຕາຍ)

Every Lao syllable is pronounced with one of the five tones, whether it has a tone mark or not. When there is no tone mark, tone rules apply. In that case, the tone is determined by consonant class and whether the syllable is live or dead.

A syllable that ends with a short vowel or a stop final consonant is called a dead syllable.

A syllable that ends with a long vowel or a sonorant final consonant is called a live syllable.

For now, just consider the short and long vowels, since we haven't introduced final consonants yet.

<u>Tone Rules for Middle Consonants</u>

In the absence of a tone mark, the tone rules for middle consonants are as follows:

Middle Consonant with <u>Live Syllable = Low Tone</u>

Middle Consonant with <u>Dead Syllable = Rising Tone</u>

Examples:

Middle Consonant + Long Vowel = Low Tone

	Sound Produced	Meaning
ก + –า	= กา (gàa)	crow
บ + ไ–	= ไบ (bpài)	to go
อ + เ–า	= เอา (ào)	to take

Reading Exercise: Read the following words and practice writing them in Lao.

1. ດີ̂ good

2. ໃຈ heart

3. ຕາ eye

4. ເກາ to scratch

5. ອາ aunt

6. ເຕາ stove

7. ບົວ lotus

8. ແຕ horn, trumpet

9. ປີ year

10. ປູ crab

11. ໄອ to cough

12. ເບຍ beer

13. ຈໍ screen

14. ໂຕ body

Middle Consonant + Short Vowel = Rising Tone

		Sound Produced	Meaning
ກ + ເ–າະ	=	ເກາະ (gɔ̌)	island
ຈ + –ະ	=	ຈະ (jǎ)	will
ຕ + ເ–ະ	=	ເຕະ (dtě)	to kick

Reading Exercise: Read the following words and practice writing them in Lao.

1. ຕິ   to criticize   2. ຊຸ   capacity

3. ບຸ   to intrude   4. ເຈາະ   to drill

5. ປະ   to leave, divorce   6. ເບາະ   cushion

7. ເກະກະ   disorderly, in the way of

Writing Exercise 2

Transcribe the following into Lao script.

1. bàa _____   11. gùa _____

2. gĕ _____   12. dtɔ̀ɔ _____

3. bʉa _____   13. ʉ̀ʉ _____

4. dtŭ _____   14. bpǎ _____

5. bɔ̀ɔ _____   15. gʉ̆ _____

6. jèe _____   16. dtŏ _____

7. gĭ _____   17. ə̀ə _____

8. jə̌ _____   18. dŏ _____

9. ɔ̀ɔ _____   19. dùa _____

10. jùa _____   20. gìa _____

Lesson 3

colors; 'jǎ' (future tense); 'dâi' (can); more
vowels; complex vowels; final consonants;
ten vowels that change their forms;
tone rules for middle consonants (cont.)

bŏt-tíi sǎam   ບົດທິ ສາມ   Lesson 3

kám-sǎp   ຄຳສັບ   Vocabulary

jǎ/si	ຈະ/ຊິ	will
dâi	ໄດ້	can
dtɛɛ	ແຕ່	but
sâa	ຊ້າ	slow
sâa-sâa	ຊ້າໆ	slowly
wái	ໄວ	quick, fast
wái-wái	ໄວໆ	quickly, fast
ìik-tɯa-nɯng	ອີກເທື່ອນຶ່ງ	one more time
het	ເຮັດ	to do, to make
kúa-gìn	ຄົວກິນ	to cook
mak	ມັກ	to like
gìn	ກິນ	to eat[1]
dɯɯm	ດື່ມ	to drink[2]
bəng	ເບິ່ງ	to watch
wâo/bpàak	ເວົ້າ/ປາກ	to speak
aan	ອ່ານ	to read
kǐan	ຂຽນ	to write
hían	ຮຽນ	to study
sɔ̌ɔn	ສອນ	to teach
het-wîak	ເຮັດວຽກ	to work
nɔ́ɔn	ນອນ	to sleep
dtɯɯn/dtɯɯn-nɔɔn		to wake up
ຕື່ນ/ ຕື່ນນອນ		
bpài	ໄປ	to go
máa	ມາ	to come
bɔɔ	ບໍ່	not
geng	ເກັ່ງ	good at

nɔ̀i-nɯng	ໜ້ອຍນື່ງ	a little
lót/lót-ñon	ລົດ/ລົດຍົນ	car
wat	ວັດ	temple
bòot	ໂບດ	church
dta-làat	ຕະຫລາດ	market
hóong-hɛ́ɛm	ໂຮງແຮມ	hotel
hóong-ngáan	ໂຮງງານ	factory
hóong-sǐi-nee-mâa	ໂຮງຊີເນມາ	movie theater
hóong-hían	ໂຮງຮຽນ	school
hóong-mɔ̌ɔ	ໂຮງໝໍ	hospital
ta-náa-káan	ທະນາຄານ	bank
bpài-sa-nii	ໄປສະນີ	post office
ma-hǎa-wi-ta-ñáa-lái		university
ມະຫາວິທະຍາໄລ		
dən-bìn	ເດີ່ນບິນ	airport
hâan-àa-hǎan	ຮ້ານອາຫານ	restaurant
àa-hǎan-waang	ອາຫານຫວ່າງ	snack
kɔ̌ɔng-wǎan	ຂອງຫວານ	dessert
nâm/nâam	ນ້ຳ	water
nâm-gɔ̂ɔn	ນ້ຳກ້ອນ	ice
nâm-màak-gîang	ນ້ຳໝາກກ້ຽງ	orange juice
gàa-fée	ກາເຟ	coffee
sáa	ຊາ	tea
bìa	ເບຍ	beer
kào	ເຂົ້າ	rice
mii/fɔ̌ə	ໝີ່/ເຝີ	noodles
àa-hǎan	ອາຫານ	food
àa-hǎan láao	ອາຫານລາວ	Lao food
àa-hǎan fa-lang	ອາຫານຝຣັ່ງ	western food
àa-hǎan jìin	ອາຫານຈີນ	Chinese food

àa-hăan ñii-bpùn   Japanese food
ອາຫານຍີ່ປຸ່ນ

kào-sao/ àa-hăan-sâo   breakfast
ເຂົ້າເຊົ້າ/ ອາຫານເຊົ້າ

kào-tiang/àa-hăan-tiang   lunch
ເຂົ້າທ່ຽງ/ ອາຫານທ່ຽງ

kào-léɛng/ àa-hăan-léɛng   dinner
ເຂົ້າແລງ/ ອາຫານແລງ

gìn-kào   ກິນເຂົ້າ   to have a meal[3]

sĭi   ສີ   color[4]

sĭi dàm   ສີດຳ   black

sĭi kăao   ສີຂາວ   white

sĭi dèɛng   ສີແດງ   red

sĭi kĭao   ສີຂຽວ   green

sĭi fâa   ສີຟ້າ   blue

sĭi fâa-gɛɛ   ສີຟ້າແກ່   dark blue

sĭi nâm-dtàan   ສີນ້ຳຕານ   brown

sĭi lŭang   ສີເຫລືອງ   yellow

sĭi bùa   ສີບົວ   pink

sĭi muang   ສີມ່ວງ   purple

sĭi sɛɛt/sĭi sôm   ສີແສດ/ ສີສົ້ມ   orange

sĭi kìi-tao   ສີຂີ້ເທົ່າ   grey

1. hap-bpa-táan (ຮັບປະທານ – to eat) is a polite form of gìn
   (ກິນ – to eat).

2. Although duum (ດື່ມ) means to drink, Lao people tend to use
   gìn (ກິນ) in less formal speech for both 'eat' and 'drink.'
   e.g. kòi mak gìn bìa. = I like to drink beer.

3. gìn-kào (ກິນເຂົ້າ) literally means "to eat rice." However, Lao
   people use this phrase for eating any main meal.

4. sĭi (ສີ) can be omitted when it is used to modify nouns.
   e.g. lot sĭi kăao = lot kăao (white car)

Conversation 1

Tongpet: jâo wâo páa-săa láao dâi bɔɔ.

ທອງເພັດ: ເຈົ້າ ເວົ້າ ພາສາ   ລາວ ໄດ້ ບໍ່?

             Can you speak Lao?

David: dâi nɔ̀i-nung.

ເດວິດ: ໄດ້   ໜ້ອຍນຶ່ງ.

             Yes, a little.

Tongpet: jâo hían páa-săa láao yuu săi.

ທອງເພັດ: ເຈົ້າ ຮຽນ   ພາສາ   ລາວ   ຢູ່ ໃສ?

             Where did you learn Lao?

David: kɔ̀i hían găp kón láao yuu àa-mée-li-gàa.

ເດວິດ: ຂ້ອຍ ຮຽນ ກັບ ຄົນ ລາວ   ຢູ່   ອາເມລິກາ.

             With Lao people in America.

Tongpet: jâo wâo láao geng lăai.

ທອງເພັດ: ເຈົ້າ ເວົ້າ ລາວ ເກັ່ງ ຫລາຍ.

             You speak Lao very well.

David: kɔ̀ɔp-jai.

ເດວິດ: ຂອບໃຈ

             Thank you.

Note: wâo páa-săa láao or wâo láao = to speak Lao

Conversation 2

Mana: jâo mak gìn àa-hǎan láao bɔɔ.

ມານະ: ເຈົ້າ ມັກ ກິນ ອາຫານ ລາວ ບໍ່?

Do you like to eat Lao food?

Paul: mak lǎai.

ປອລ: ມັກ ຫລາຍ.

Yes, I like it very much.

jâo mak àa-hǎan fa-lang bɔɔ.

ເຈົ້າ ມັກ ອາຫານ ຝຣັ່ງ ບໍ່?

Do you like western food?

Mana: kɔ̀i bɔɔ mak. kɔ̀i mak àa-hǎan ñii-bpun.

ມານະ: ຂ້ອຍ ບໍ່ ມັກ. ຂ້ອຍ ມັກ ອາຫານ ຍີ່ປຸ່ນ.

No, I don't. I like Japanese food.

jâo jǎ dɯ̯ɯm sáa lɯ̀ɯ-waa gàa-fée.

ເຈົ້າ ຈະ ກິ່ມ ຊາ ຫລືວ່າ ກາເຟ?

Will you drink tea or coffee?

Paul: jǎ dɯ̯ɯm gàa-fée.

ປອລ: ຈະ ກິ່ມ ກາເຟ.

I will drink coffee.

bpà-ñòok   ปะໄທຍກ   Sentences

1. A: jâo (bɔɔ) mak   àa-hǎan ñǎng.
      ເຈົ້າ (ບໍ່) ມັກ   ອາຫານ ຫຍັງ?
      What food do (don't) you like?

    B: kɔ̀i (bɔɔ) mak àa-hǎan láao.
      ຂ້ອຍ (ບໍ່) ມັກ   ອາຫານ ລາວ.
      I (don't) like Lao food.

    C: jâo (bɔɔ) mak sǐi ñǎng.
      ເຈົ້າ (ບໍ່) ມັກ   ສີ ຫຍັງ?
      What color do (don't) you like?

    D: kɔ̀i (bɔɔ) mak sǐi kǎao.
      ຂ້ອຍ (ບໍ່) ມັກ   ສີ ຂາວ.
      I (don't) like white.

    E: jâo (bɔɔ) mak het ñǎng.
      ເຈົ້າ (ບໍ່) ມັກ   ເຮັດ ຫຍັງ?
      What do (don't) you like to do?

    F: kɔ̀i (bɔɔ) mak bəng tóo-la-tat.
      ຂ້ອຍ (ບໍ່) ມັກ   ເບິ່ງ ໂທລະທັດ.
      I (don't) like watching TV.

2. A: jâo mak àa-hǎan jìin bɔɔ.
      ເຈົ້າ ມັກ ອາຫານ   ຈີນ ບໍ່?
      Do you like Chinese food?

    B: mak.
      ມັກ.
      Yes, I do.

    C: bɔɔ mak.
      ບໍ່ ມັກ.
      No, I don't.

3. A: jâo mak àa-hǎan láao lǔu àa-hǎan fa-lang.

ເຈົ້າ ມັກ ອາຫານ ລາວ ຫຼື ອາຫານ ຝຣັ່ງ?

Do you like Lao food or western food?

B: kòi mak àa-hǎan láao.

ຂ້ອຍ ມັກ ອາຫານ ລາວ.

I like Lao food.

C: jâo mak lot sǐi kǎao lǔu lot sǐi dèɛng.

ເຈົ້າ ມັກ ລົດ ສີ ຂາວ ຫຼື ລົດ ສີ ແດງ?

Do you like white cars or red cars?

D: kòi mak lot sǐi dèɛng.

ຂ້ອຍ ມັກ ລົດ ສີ ແດງ.

I like red cars.

4. A: jâo aan páa-sǎa láao dâi bɔɔ.

ເຈົ້າ ອ່ານ ພາສາ ລາວ ໄດ້ ບໍ່?

Can you read Lao?

B: dâi.

ໄດ້

Yes, I can.

C: bɔɔ dâi.

ບໍ່ ໄດ້.

No, I can't.

5. A: jâo kǐan páa-sǎa láao dâi bɔɔ.

ເຈົ້າ ຂຽນ ພາສາ ລາວ ໄດ້ ບໍ່?

Can you write in Lao?

B: bɔɔ dâi. dtɛɛ aan dâi nòi-nung.

ບໍ່ ໄດ້. ແຕ່ ອ່ານ ໄດ້ ໜ້ອຍນຶ່ງ.

No, I can't. But I can read a little.

6. A: jâo ja bpài sǎi.

ເຈົ້າ ຈະ ໄປ ໃສ?

Where will you go?

B: jà bpài hâan-àa-hǎan láao.

ຈະ ໄປ ຮ້ານອາຫານ ລາວ.

I will go to a Lao restaurant.

C: ja bpài dɔn-bìn.

ຈະ ໄປ ເດີ່ນບິນ.

I will go to the airport.

7. A: láao mak dɯɯm ñăng.

ລາວ ມັກ ດື່ມ ຫຍັງ?

What does he/she like to drink?

B: láao mak dɯɯm gàa-fée.

ລາວ ມັກ ດື່ມ ກາເຝ.

He/she likes to drink coffee.

C: láao mak dɯɯm bia láao.

ລາວ ມັກ ດື່ມ ເບຍ ລາວ.

He/she likes to drink Lao beer.

8. A: jâo het wîak yuu săi.

ເຈົ້າ ເຮັດ ວຽກ ຢູ່ ໃສ?

Where do you work?

B: kɔ̀i het wîak yuu wîang-jàn.

ຂ້ອຍ ເຮັດ ວຽກ ຢູ່ ວຽງຈັນ.

I work in Vientiane.

C: jâo ja gìn kào-tiang yuu săi.

ເຈົ້າ ຈະ ກິນ ເຂົ້າ-ທ່ຽງ ຢູ່ ໃສ?

Where will you have lunch?

D: yuu hâan-àa-hăan láao.

ຢູ່ ຮ້ານອາຫານ ລາວ.

At a Lao restaurant.

9. kɔ̆ɔ-tôot. wâo sâa-sâa dâi bɔɔ.

ຂໍ ໂທດ. ເວົ້າ ຊ້າໆ ໄດ້ ບໍ່?

Excuse me. Could you speak slowly?

10. wâo (kɯ̀ɯn) ìik-tɯa-nɯng dâi bɔɔ.

ເວົ້າ (ຄືນ) ອີກເທື່ອນຶ່ງ ໄດ້ ບໍ່?

Can you say that again?

Test 3

Match the English words with the Lao words.

_____ 1. school   a. wat ວັດ

_____ 2. eat   b. sǐi dàm ສີດຳ

_____ 3. airport   c. bəng ເບິ່ງ

_____ 4. temple   d. sǐi kǎao ສີຂາວ

_____ 5. to speak   e. lot ລົດ

_____ 6. food   f. dən-bìn ເດິ່ນບິນ

_____ 7. black   g. sǐi dèeng ສີແດງ

_____ 8. rice   h. het ເຮັດ

_____ 9. white   i. ma-hǎa-wi-ta-ñáa-lái
                              ມະຫາວິທະຍາໄລ

_____ 10. tea   j. hóong-hían ໂຮງຮຽນ

_____ 11. to watch   k. àa-hǎan-waang ອາຫານຫວ່າງ

_____ 12. car   l. kào ເຂົ້າ

_____ 13. to do, to make   m. àa-hǎan ອາຫານ

_____ 14. university   n. gìn ກິນ

_____ 15. snack   o. aan ອ່ານ

                                p. sáa ຊາ

                                q. wâo ເວົ້າ

                                r. hóong-sǐi-nee-mâa ໂຮງຊີເນມາ

Translate the following into English.

1. jâo het wîak yuu săi.

   ເຈົ້າ ເຮັດ ວຽກ ຢູ່ ໃສ?

   _____

2. kɔ̀i mak lot sĭi fâa.

   ຂ້ອຍ ມັກ ລົດ ສີ ຟ້າ.

   _____

3. jâo mak àa-hăan láao lʉ̈ʉ àa-hăan jìin.

   ເຈົ້າ ມັກ ອາຫານ ລາວ ຫລື ອາຫານ ຈີນ.

   _____

4. jâo jă bpai sai.

   ເຈົ້າ ຈະ ໄປ ໃສ?

   _____

5. jâo kĭan páa-săa láao dâi geng lăai.

   ເຈົ້າ ຂຽນ ພາສາ ລາວ ໄດ້ ເກັ່ງ ຫລາຍ.

   _____

More Vowels

The following vowels may sound either short or long (mostly short), but are categorized as long vowels for tone rule purposes.

$-°\gamma$ /àm/

$\complement-$ /ài/ (mái-múan)

$\complement-$ /ài/ (mái-má-lai)

$\complement-\gamma$ /ào/

$\complement-$ and $\complement-$ are pronounced the same. You need to memorize which one is used with a particular word.

Complex Vowels

The following can be considered complex vowels. They are vowels followed by the sonorant consonants ບ or ຽ and ວ .

$-\gamma$ບ   /àai/

$-\S$ວ   /iao/

ເ–ຍ /ìa/ is sometimes spelled ເ–ັຍ or ເ–ຽ.

–າວ /àao/

–ວຍ /ùai/

ເ–ືອຍ /ʉ̀ai/

–ອຍ /ɔɔi/

ໂ–ຍ /ooi/

–ຸຍ /ui/

–ິວ /iu/

ເ–ວ /eeo/

ແ–ວ /ɛɛo/

ເ–ີຍ /əəi/

Practice Writing the Following Vowels

Use ອ /-/ as the consonant when practicing the following vowels.

ອຳ   ອຳ   ອຳ

ໃອ   ໃອ   ໃອ

ອາຍ   ອາຍ   ອາຍ

ອຽວ   ອຽວ   ອຽວ

ອາວ   ອາວ   ອາວ

ອວຍ   ອວຍ   ອວຍ

ເຄື້ອຍ ເອືອຍ ເອືອຍ

ອອຍ ອອຍ ອອຍ

ໂອຍ ໂອຍ ໂອຍ

ອູຍ ອູຍ ອູຍ

ອິວ ອິວ ອິວ

ເອວ ເອວ ເອວ

ແອວ ແອວ ແອວ

ເອືຍ ເອືຍ ເອືຍ

Read The Following Aloud

1. ກຳ ໃກ ໄກ ເກົາ ເກຶຍ

2. ຈຳ ໃຈ ໄຈ ເຈົາ ເຈຶຍ

3. ຄຳ ໃຄ ໄຄ ເຄົາ ເຄຶຍ

4. ຕຳ ໃຕ ໄຕ ເຕົາ ເຕຶຍ

5. ບຳ ໃບ ໄບ ເບົາ ເບຶຍ

6. ປຳ ໃປ ໄປ ເປົາ ເປຶຍ

7. ອຳ ໃອ ໄອ ເອົາ ເອຶຍ

8. ກຳ ກ່ຳ ກ້ຳ

9. ໃຈ ໃຈ່ ໃຈ້

10. ໄກ ໄກ່ ໄກ້

11. ເຕົາ ເຕົ່າ ເຕົ້າ

12. ເບຶຍ ເບຶ່ຍ ເບຶ້ຍ

Final Consonants

There are eight final consonant sounds which can end a syllable. They are divided into two categories: sonorant and stop. Sonorant finals are voiced. If you touch your larynx (voice box) while pronouncing them, you will feel a vibration. Stop finals are unvoiced. The five sonorant and three stop finals are most commonly written as follows:

Sonorant Finals (All Low Consonants)

ຈ	ຈ ຈົວ	ngóɔ ngúa (cow)	/ng/
ໜ	ໜ ໜົກ	nɔ́ɔ nok (bird)	/n/
ມ	ມ ແມວ	mɔ́ɔ mέεɔ (cat)	/m/
ຍ	ຍ ຍູງ	ñɔ́ɔ ñúng (mosquito)	/ñ/
ວ	ວ ວີ	wɔ́ɔ wíi (fan)	/w/

Stop Finals (All Mid Consonants)

ກ	ກ ໄກ່	gɔ̀ɔ gai (chicken)	/k/
ດ	ດ ເດັກ	dɔ̀ɔ děk (child)	/t/
ບ	ບ ແບ້	bɔ̀ɔ bε̂ε (goat)	/p/

Notes: 1. When ກ , ດ, ບ and ຍ are initial consonants, they are transcribed as /g-/, /d-/, /b-/ and /ñ or ny/ respectively. However, when they are final consonants, they are transcribed as /-k/, /-t/, /-p/ and /-i/.

2. ວ forms part of the vowels -ົວ and ◌ົ◌, which are transcribed as /àao/ and /ùa/ respectively. ◌ິວ is transcribed as /ìu/ and –ຽວ is transcribed as /ìao/.

Practice Writing the
Following Consonants

The following consonants are written with one stroke.
Start near the ❶.

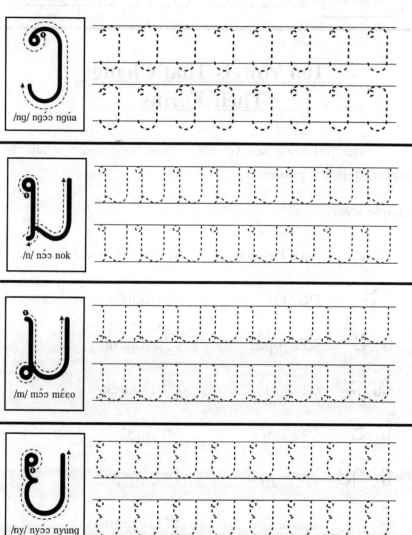

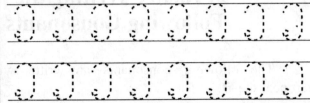

/w/ wɔ́ɔ wíi

Ten Vowels That Change Their Forms

The following ten vowels change their forms when they appear in medial position.

Simple Vowels

Vowels	Final Position	Medial Position
◌ະ	ກະ /gǎ/	ກັດ /gǎt/
ເ◌ະ	ເປະ /bpě/	ເປັນ /bpèn/
ແ◌ະ	ແຕະ /dě/	ແຕກ /dtěk/
ໂ◌ະ	ໂຈະ /jǒ/	ຈິບ /jǒp/
ເ◌າະ	ເກາະ /gɔ̌/	ກັອບ /gɔ̌p/
◌ໍ	ສໍ /sɔ̌/	ສອນ /sɔ̌ɔn/

Diphthongs

Vowels	Final Position	Medial Position
ເ◌ັຍະ	ເຈັຍະ /jǐa/	ຈຽກ /jǐak/
ເ◌ຍ	ເສຍ /sǐa/	ສຽນ /sǐan/
◌ົວະ	ຕົວະ /dtǔa/	ຕົວນ /dtǔan/
◌ົວ	ມົວ /múa/	ມວນ /múan/

Special Vowel Alternatives

In the old Lao writing system, you may encounter some of the following alternative forms of these special vowels.

ໄ◌	/ài/	↔	◌ັຍ	/ài/
ໃ◌	/ài/	↔	◌ັຍ	/ài/
◌ຳ	/àm/	↔	◌ັມ	/àm/

Live and Dead Syllables

To review, here are the rules for live and dead syllables:

A syllable that ends with a short vowel or a stop final consonant is called a <u>dead syllable</u>.

A syllable that ends with a long vowel or a sonorant final consonant is called a <u>live syllable</u>.

Rising tone and its corresponding tone mark $\left(^{+}_{-} \right)$ never occur with a dead syllable.

<u>Tone Rules for Middle Consonants</u> (cont.)

In the absence of a tone mark, the tone rules for middle consonants are as follows:

Middle Consonant with <u>Live Syllable = Low Tone</u>

Middle Consonant with <u>Dead Syllable = Rising Tone</u>

Examples:

Middle Consonant + Any Vowel + <u>Sonorant Final</u>
    = Low Tone

		<u>Sound Produced</u>	<u>Meaning</u>
ก + ◌ิ + น	=	กิน (gìn)	to eat
จ + ◌ิ + ง	=	จิง (jùng)	therefore
ด + เ- + ย	=	เดย (dòoi)	by

Middle Consonant + Short Vowel + <u>Stop Final</u>
   = Rising Tone

	<u>Sound Produced</u>	<u>Meaning</u>
ກ + ະ + ບ	= ກັບ (gǎp)	with, and
ປ + ◌ົ + ດ	= ປິດ (bpǐt)	to close
ຈ + ◌ັ + ກ	= ຈັກ (jǎk)	sewing machine

Reading Exercise: Read the following words and practice writing them in Lao. Also identify the tones.

1. ແອວ waist

2. ແອບ to practice

3. ຕາມ to follow

4. ຈອດ to park

5. ອາບ to bathe

6. ເກີນ to exceed

7. ຈັດ to arrange

8. ຕົກ to fall

9. ຕາຍ to die

10. ຈົບ to be finished

11. ປົນ to mix

12. ບຸກ to invade

13. ຕຽງ bed

14. ບານ to blossom

Writing Exercise 3

Transcribe the following into Lao script. Notice that most of the vowels are in medial position and must change forms accordingly.

1. jàn _____

11. dòn _____

2. bpə̀ət _____

12. èn _____

3. bàng _____

13. dὲm _____

4. gùam _____

14. jừng _____

5. jừut _____

15. bùam _____

6. dtὲm _____

16. òng _____

7. pŏm _____

17. də̀ən _____

8. dàng _____

18. jĕp _____

9. gĕp _____

19. bpùat _____

10. dŏk _____

20. bùak _____

Transcribe the following into Lao script using appropriate tone marks.

21. gân _____   31. dtăn _____

22. jom _____   32. bìip _____

23. bâng _____   33. dâng _____

24. ùut _____   34. băt _____

25. gûng _____   35. bàai _____

26. jàam _____   36. oong _____

27. gao _____   37. jăa _____

28. dtɰɰn _____   38. jèp _____

29. dâam _____   39. gɛ̀ɛp _____

30. ôok _____   40. jăao _____

Lesson 4

telling time; high consonants; tone rules for high consonants

bŏt-tíi sii   ບົດທີ ສີ່   Lesson 4

kám-săp   ຄຳສັບ   Vocabulary

wée-láa	ເວລາ	time
sua-móong	ຊົ່ວໂມງ	hour
náa-tíi	ນາທີ	minute
wi-náa-tíi	ວິນາທີ	second
dtòng/gòng	ຕົງ/ກົງ	exactly
kəng	ເຄິ່ງ	half
gùap	ເກືອບ	almost
bpàai	ປາຍ	past
lɛ̂ɛo	ແລ້ວ	already
bpa-máan	ປະມານ	about
ìik	ອິກ	more, again
ìik hàa náa-tíi	ອິກຫ້ານາທີ	five more minutes
sâa	ຊ້າ	slow
wái/sâo	ໄວ/ເຊົ້າ	fast, early
sŭai	ສວຍ	late
gɔɔn	ກ່ອນ	before
lăng	ຫລັງ	after
dtɔ̀ɔn	ຕອນ	at, when
dtɔ̀ɔn sâo	ຕອນເຊົ້າ	in the morning
dtɔ̀ɔn ngáai/dtɔ̀ɔn sŭai		late morning
ຕອນງາຍ/ຕອນສວຍ		
dtɔ̀ɔn tiang	ຕອນທ່ຽງ	at noon
dtɔ̀ɔn baai	ຕອນບ່າຍ	in the afternoon
dtɔ̀ɔn lɛ́ɛng	ຕອນແລງ	in the evening
dtɔ̀ɔn kam	ຕອນຄຳ	at night
dtɔ̀ɔn dək	ຕອນດຶກ	late at night
dìao-nîi/dtɔ̀ɔn nîi	ດຽວນີ້/ຕອນນີ້	now

waang-gîi-nîi   ຫວ່າງກີ້ນີ້   just now
ñáam-dai   ຍາມໃດ   when
jàak/dtεε   ຈາກ/ແຕ່   from
tăng/hăa/hôot   ເຖິງ/ຫາ/ຮອດ   to, until

wée-láa   ເວລາ   **Time**

jăk móong (lêεo)   What time is it?
ຈັກໂມງ (ແລ້ວ) ?

a.m.   1:00   nung móong ນຶ່ງໂມງ
       2:00   sɔ̆ɔng móong ສອງໂມງ
       3:00   săam móong ສາມໂມງ
       4:00   sii móong ສີໂມງ
       5:00   hàa móong ຫ້າໂມງ
       6:00   hŏk móong (sâo) ຫົກໂມງ (ເຊົ້າ)
       7:00   jĕt móong (sâo) ເຈັດໂມງ (ເຊົ້າ)
       8:00   bpεεt móong (sâo) ແປດໂມງ (ເຊົ້າ)
       9:00   gâo móong (sâo) ເກົ້າໂມງ (ເຊົ້າ)
       10:00 sĭp móong (sâo) ສິບໂມງ (ເຊົ້າ)
       11:00 sĭp-ĕt móong (sâo) ສິບເອັດໂມງ (ເຊົ້າ)

p.m.   12:00   tiang/tiang-dtòng/sǐp sɔ̌ɔng móong
                  ທ່ຽງ/ ທ່ຽງຕົງ/ ສິບສອງໂມງ

        1:00   baai nɯng (móong)/baai móong
                  ບ່າຍນຶ່ງ (ໂມງ) / ບ່າຍໂມງ

        2:00   (baai) sɔ̌ɔng móong (ບ່າຍ) ສອງໂມງ

        3:00   (baai) sǎam móong (ບ່າຍ) ສາມໂມງ

        4:00   (baai) sìi móong (ບ່າຍ) ສີ່ໂມງ

        5:00   (baai) hàa móong (ບ່າຍ) ຫ້າໂມງ

        6:00   hǒk móong (lɛ́ɛng) ຫົກໂມງ (ແລງ)

        7:00   jĕt móong ເຈັດໂມງ (ແລງ)

        8:00   bpɛ̀ɛt móong ແປດໂມງ (ແລງ)

        9:00   gâo móong ເກົ້າໂມງ (ແລງ)

      10:00   sǐp móong ສິບໂມງ (ແລງ)

      11:00   sǐp ĕt móong ສິບເອັດໂມງ (ແລງ)

a.m.   12:00   sǐp sɔ̌ɔng móong gang kʉʉn/tîang-kʉʉn
                  ສິບສອງໂມງກາງຄືນ/ ທ່ຽງຄືນ

Conversation

Kampong: jâo dtɯɯn jǎk móong.

ຄຳພົງ: ເຈົ້າ ຕື່ນ ຈັກ ໂມງ?

              What time do you get up?

Pakong: bpa-máan jĕt móong sâo.

ປະຄອງ: ປະມານ ເຈັດ ໂມງ ເຊົ້າ.

              About seven o'clock.

Kampong: gɔɔn bpài gàan jâo het ñang dɛɛ.

ຄຳພົງ: ກ່ອນ ໄປ ການ ເຈົ້າ ເຮັດ ຫຍັງ ແດ່?

              What do you do before going to work?

Pakong: kɔ̀i gìn kào sâo lɛ aan nǎng-sɯ̌ɯ-pím.

ປະຄອງ: ຂ້ອຍ ກິນ ເຂົ້າ ເຊົ້າ ແລະ ອ່ານ ຫນັງສືພິມ.

              I make breakfast and read the paper.

Kampong: jâo nɔ́ɔn jǎk móong.

ຄຳພົງ: ເຈົ້າ ນອນ ຈັກ ໂມງ?

              What time do you go to bed?

Pakong: gàai tiang-kɯɯn bpài nɔ̀i-nɯng.

ປະຄອງ: ກາຍ ທ່ຽງຄືນ ໄປ ຫນ້ອຍນຶ່ງ.

              A little after midnight.

bpà-ñòok   ປະໂຫຍກ   Sentences

1. A: dtɔ̀ɔn nîi jăk móong (lɛ̂ɛo).

   ຕອນ ນີ້ ຈັກ ໂມງ (ແລ້ວ) ?

   What time is it now?

   B: dtɔ̀ɔn nîi baai hàa móong.

   ຕອນ ນີ້ ບ່າຍ ຫ້າ ໂມງ.

   It's now five p.m.

   C: dtɔ̀ɔn nîi ´ tiang kəng.

   ຕອນ ນີ້ ທ່ຽງ ເຄິ່ງ.

   It's now half past twelve noon.

   D: dtɔ̀ɔn nîi gâao móong bpàai nɔ̀i-nung.

   ຕອນ ນີ້ ເກົ້າ ໂມງ ປາຍ ໜ້ອຍນຶ່ງ.

   It's now a little past nine a.m.

   E: dtɔ̀ɔn nîi baai sɔ̌ɔng móong dtòng.

   ຕອນ ນີ້ ບ່າຍ ສອງ ໂມງ ຕົງ.

   It's now exactly two p.m.

   F: dtɔ̀ɔn nîi săam móong bpàai sĭp.

   ຕອນ ນີ້ ສາມ ໂມງ ປາຍ ສິບ.

   It's now ten minutes after three.

   G: dtɔ̀ɔn nîi sĭp ĕt móong saao.

   ຕອນ ນີ້ ສິບ ເອັດ ໂມງ ຊາວ.

   It's now twenty past eleven.

   H: dtɔ̀ɔn nîi nung móong kəng.

   ຕອນ ນີ້ ນຶ່ງ ໂມງ ເຄິ່ງ.

   It's now half past one a.m.

2. A: jâo gìn kào léeng jăk móong.

    ເຈົ້າ ກິນ ເຂົ້າ ແລງ ຈັກ ໂມງ?

    What time do you eat dinner?

    B: kɔ̀i gìn kào léeng (dtɔ̀ɔn)* hŏk móong.

    ຂ້ອຍ ກິນ ເຂົ້າ ແລງ (ຕອນ) ຫົກ ໂມງ.

    I eat dinner at six.

    C: jâo bpài wîak jăk móong.

    ເຈົ້າ ໄປ ວຽກ ຈັກ ໂມງ?

    What time do you go to work?

    D: kɔ̀i bpài wîak (dtɔ̀ɔn)* bpὲet móong.

    ຂ້ອຍ ໄປ ວຽກ (ຕອນ) ແປດ ໂມງ.

    I go to work at eight.

    E: jâo jă bəng tóo-la-tat jăk móong.

    ເຈົ້າ ຈະ ເບິ່ງ ໂທລະທັດ ຈັກ ໂມງ?

    What time will you watch TV?

    F: kɔ̀i jă bəng tóo-la-tat dtɔ̀ɔn dŏk.

    ຂ້ອຍ ຈະ ເບິ່ງ ໂທລະທັດ ຕອນ ດຶກ.

    I will watch TV late at night.

    * dtɔ̀ɔn can be omitted in these sentences.

3. A: hàa móong dtòng.

    ຫ້າ ໂມງ ຕົງ.

    Exactly 5 p.m.

    B: hàa móong bpàai.

    ຫ້າ ໂມງ ປາຍ.

    Past 5 p.m.

    C: hàa móong léeng lêeo.

    ຫ້າ ໂມງ ແລງ ແລ້ວ.

    Already 5 p.m.

D: bpa-máan hàa móong.

ປະມານ   ຫ້າ ໂມງ

Around 5 p.m.

E: gùap hàa móong.

ເກືອບ ຫ້າ ໂມງ

Almost 5 p.m.

F: hàa móong ñáng sǐp.

ຫ້າ ໂມງ ຍັງ ສິບ.

Ten minutes to 5 p.m.

G: hàa móong bpàai hàa náa-tíi.

ຫ້າ ໂມງ ປາຍ ຫ້າ ມາທີ.

Five minutes past 5 p.m.

H: hàa móong bpàai sǐp.

ຫ້າ ໂມງ ປາຍ ສິບ.

Ten past 5 p.m.

I: hàa móong kəng.

ຫ້າ ໂມງ ເຄິ່ງ.

Half past 5 p.m.

4.   A: láao máa sâa-sâa.

ລາວ ມາ ຊ້າໆ.

He came slowly.

B: láao máa wái.

ລາວ ມາ ໄວ.

He came early.

C: láao máa sǔai.

ລາວ ມາ ສວຍ.

He came late.

5. kɔ̀i hǐan páa-sǎa láao dtɛɛ baai móong tǔng baai sii móong.

ຂ້ອຍ ຮຽນ ພາສາ   ລາວ ແຕ່ ບ່າຍ ໂມງ   ເຖິງ ບ່າຍ ສີ່ ໂມງ.

I study Lao from one p.m to four p.m.

6. A: jâo hǐan páa-sǎa láao jǎk sua-móong.

ເຈົ້າ ຮຽນ   ພາສາ ລາວ ຈັກ   ຊົ່ວໂມງ?

How many hours do you study Lao?

B: kɔ̀i hǐan páa-sǎa láao sǎam sua-móong.

ຂ້ອຍ ຮຽນ   ພາສາ ລາວ ສາມ   ຊົ່ວໂມງ.

We study Lao for three hours.

7. A: jâo lɔ̂əm aan bpûm dtɛɛ dtɔ̀ɔn jǎk móong.

ເຈົ້າ ເລີ້ມ ອ່ານ ປຶ້ມ   ແຕ່ ຕອນ ຈັກ ໂມງ?

When did you start reading?

B: kɔ̀i lɔ̂m aan bpûm dtɛɛ dtɔ̀ɔn gâo móong lɛ́ɛng.

ຂ້ອຍ ເລີ້ມ ອ່ານ ປຶ້ມ   ແຕ່ ຕອນ ເກົ້າ ໂມງ ແລງ.

I've been reading since nine p.m.

aan bpûm literally means " to read a book." It also
means "to read" in general.

8. láao ja bpài dən-bìn dtɔ̀ɔn baai sǎam móong.

ລາວ ຈະ ໄປ   ເດີ່ນ-ບິນ ຕອນ ບ່າຍ ສາມ ໂມງ.

He will go to the airport at three p.m.

9. dtɔ̀ɔn tiang kɔ̀i ja het àa hǎan láao.

ຕອນ ທ່ຽງ   ຂ້ອຍ ຈະ ເຮັດ ອາຫານ ລາວ.

I will make Lao food at noon.

10. kɔ̀i ja bpài hɔ̀ng-nâm hàa náa-tii.

ຂ້ອຍ ຈະ ໄປ   ຫ້ອງນ້ຳ   ຫ້າ ນາທີ.

I will go to the bathroom for five minutes.

11. kɔ̀i het wîak hàa sua-móong kəng.

ຂ້ອຍ ເຮັດ ວຽກ ຫ້າ   ຊົ່ວໂມງ ເຄິ່ງ.

I work for five and a half hours.

12.   ìik sǐp náa-tíi kɔ̀i ja tóo máa hǎa jâo.

ອີກ ສິບ ນາທີ ຂ້ອຍ ຈະ ໂທ ມາ ຫາ ເຈົ້າ.

I will give you a call in ten minutes.

13.   kɔ̀i het-wîak dtεε sâo hɔ̀ɔt tiang.

ຂ້ອຍ ເຮັດວຽກ ແຕ່ ເຊົ້າ ຣອດ ທ່ຽງ.

I work from morning till noon.

14. A: jâo ja bpài ta-náa-káan ñáam dǎi.

ເຈົ້າ ຈະ ໄປ ທະນາຄານ ຍາມ ໃດ?

When will you go to the bank?

    B: dtɔ̀ɔn baai.

ຕອນ ບ່າຍ.

In the afternoon.

Test 4

Tell what time it is indicating a.m. or p.m. (Use either a.m or p.m., but if you want to write both when there is more than one answer, that's fine also.) Look at the example.

Example: sǎam móong =   3:00 p.m./3:00 a.m.

1. hǒk móong sǐp hàa. ຫົກໂມງສິບຫ້າ. _____

2. baai sǎam. ບ່າຍສາມ. _____

3. sii móong kɔ̀ng. ສີ່ໂມງຄີ່ງ. _____

4. sɔ̌ɔng móong sǎam sǐp hàa. ສອງໂມງສິບຫ້າ. _____

5. baai sǎam móong gɔ̀ng. ບ່າຍສາມໂມງກີ່ງ. _____

6. hàa móong ñáng sǐp. ຫ້າໂມງຍ້ງສິບ. _____

7. sǐp sɔ̌ɔng móong sáao. ສິບສອງໂມງຂາວ. _____

8. baai nɯng móong hàa náa-tíi. ບ່າຍນຶ່ງໂມງຫ້ານາທີ. _____

9. bpɛ̀ɛt móong sáao náa-tíi. ແປດໂມງຂາວນາທີ. _____

10. sii móong sâo. ສີ່ໂມງເຊົ້າ. _____

11. sǐp móong sâo. ສິບໂມງເຊົ້າ. _____

12. tiang dtɔ̀ng. ທ່ຽງຕ້ງ. _____

13. bpɛ̀ɛt móong lɛ́ɛng. ແປດໂມງແລງ. _____

14. bpɛ̀ɛt móong sǐp. ແປດໂມງສິບ. _____

15. hàa móong sâo. ຫ້າໂມງເຊົ້າ. _____

Translate the following into English.

1. kɔ̀i   sì bpài   wat   dtɔ̀ɔn tiang.
    ຂ້ອຍ ສິ ໄປ   ວັດ   ຕອນ ທ່ຽງ.

    _____

2. láao aan bpûm dtâng-dtɛɛ sǐp-ĕt móong lɛ́ɛng.
    ລາວ ອ່ານ ປຶ້ມ   ຕັ້ງແຕ່   ສິບເອັດ ໂມງ ແລງ.

    _____

3. háo hían páa-sǎa láao sǎam sua-móong.
    ເຮົາ ຮຽນ ພາສາ   ລາວ ສາມ ຊົ່ວໂມງ.

    _____

4. dtɔ̀ɔn nîi wée-láa baai móong kəng.
    ຕອນ ນີ້ ເວລາ   ບ່າຍ ໂມງ ເຄິ່ງ.

    _____

5. kɔ̀i gìn kào-sâo dtɔ̀ɔn bpɛ̀ɛt móong.
    ຂ້ອຍ ກິນ ເຂົ້າເຊົ້າ ຕອນ ແປດ ໂມງ.

    _____

High Consonants

ອັກສອນສູງ (ăk-sɔ̌ɔn-sǔung)

There are six "high" consonants in Lao as follows:

Consonant		Consonant Name	Sound
ຂ	ຂ ໄຂ່	kɔ̌ɔ kai - egg	/k/
ສ	ສ ເສືອ	sɔ̌ɔ sǔa - tiger	/s/
ຕ	ຕ ຖົງ	tɔ̌ɔ tǒng - bag	/t/
ຜ	ຜ ເຜິ້ງ	pɔ̌ɔ pɔ̀ng - bee	/p/
ຝ	ຝ ຝົນ	fɔ̌ɔ fǒn - rain	/f/
ຫ	ຫ ຫ່ານ	hɔ̌ɔ haan - goose	/h/

Practice Writing the High Consonants

Notice that you always start with a small circle where there is one. Start near the ❶.

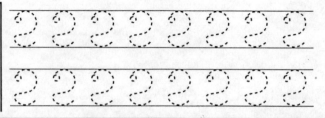

/k/ kɔ̌ɔ kai

/s/ sɔ̌ɔ sǔa

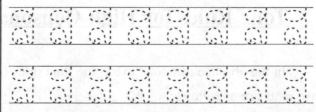

/t/ tɔ̌ɔ tǒng

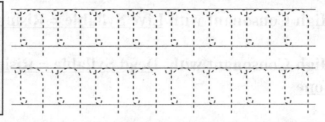

/p/ pɔ̌ɔ pèng

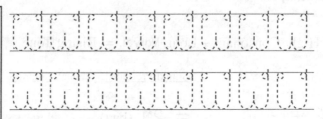

/f/ fɔ̌ɔ fǒn

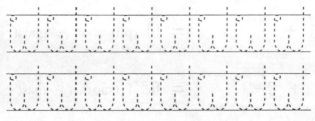

/h/ hɔ̌ɔ hǎan

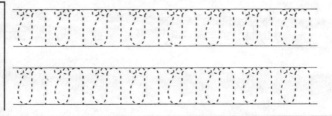

Tone Rules for High Consonants

In the absence of a tone mark, the tone rules for high consonants are as follows:

High Consonant with Live Syllable = Rising Tone

High Consonant with Dead Syllable = Rising or Low Tone

Examples:

High Consonant + Long Vowel = Rising Tone

	Sound Produced	Meaning
ຂ + −ๅ	= ຂๅ (kǎa)	leg
ຜ + ◌ີ	= ຜີ (pǐi)	ghost
ເ + ເ−ๅ	= ເສົๅ (sǎo)	mast

Reading Exercise: Read the following words and practice writing them in Lao.

1. ຫົວ head   2. ເສືອ tiger

3. ໄຝ mole   4. ຫູ ear

5. ແຂນ arm   6. ຜົວ husband

7. ສີ color   8. ຫາ to look for

9. ຝາ lid   10. ສາມ three

High Consonant + Short Vowel = Rising Tone

	Sound Produced	Meaning
ສ + –ະ	= ສະ (sǎ)	pond
ຫ + ເ–າະ	= ເຫາະ (hǒ)	to fly e.g. Superman

Reading Exercise: Read the following words and practice writing them in Lao.

1. ຜຸ rotten

2. ສະຫະ united

3. ສິວ name of a god, mountain (Sanskrit)

High Consonant + Any Vowel + <u>Sonorant Final</u> = Rising Tone

<u>Sound Produced</u>   <u>Meaning</u>

ຂ + ◌ັ + ນ = ຂັນ (kǎn)   to crow, to coo

ສ + −າ + ນ = ສານ (sǎam)   three

ຖ + ◌ັ + ງ = ຖັງ (tǒng)   sack

High Consonant + Short Vowel + <u>Stop Final</u> = Rising Tone

<u>Sound Produced</u>   <u>Meaning</u>

ຂ + ◌ັ + ບ = ຂັບ (kǎp)   to drive

ຜ + ◌ິ + ດ = ຜິດ (pǐt)   wrong

ຖ + ◌ັ + ກ = ຖັກ (tùuk)   correct

High Consonant + Long Vowel + <u>Stop Final</u> = Low Tone

<u>Sound Produced</u>   <u>Meaning</u>

ຜ + −າ + ກ = ຜາກ (fàak)   to deposit

ສ + ◌ູ + ບ = ສູບ (sùup)   to smoke, pump

ຫ + ໂ− + ດ = ໂຫດ (hòot)   cruel

Reading Exercise: Read the following words and practice writing them in Lao. Also identify the tones.

1. ສູງ tall

2. ເຕີງ to

3. ຫາດ beach

4. ຜົມ hair

5. ສຸກ ripe

6. ແຂກ guest

7. ຫົກ six

8. ຖານ base

9. ເຂີຍ son-in-law

10. ສິບ ten

11. ສາຍ line

12. ຂັງ to detain

Writing Exercise 4

Transcribe the following into Lao script.

1. săa _____   8. hŭp _____

2. pǎ _____   9. tŭng _____

3. sàak _____   10. pŏng _____

4. kùut _____   11. făn _____

5. sĭao _____   12. hàap _____

6. fĭi _____   13. fàat _____

7. hὲεk _____   14. fŭung _____

Lesson 5

days of the week; months; tone marks with high consonants; low consonants introduced

bŏt-tíi hàa   ບົດທິ ຫ້າ   Lesson 5

kám-săp   ຄຳສັບ   Vocabulary

wán	ວັນ	day
wán-àa-tit	ວັນອາທິດ	Sunday[1]
wán-jàn	ວັນຈັນ	Monday
wán-àng-káan	ວັນອັງຄານ	Tuesday
wán-put	ວັນພຸດ	Wednesday
wán-pa-hăt	ວັນພະຫັດ	Thursday
wán-sŭk	ວັນສຸກ	Friday
wán-săo	ວັນເສົາ	Saturday
wán-pak	ວັນພັກ	holiday
săo-àa-tit	ເສົາອາທິດ	weekend
dùan	ເດືອນ	month
máng-gɔɔ̀n	ມັງກອນ	January[2]
gùm-páa	ກຸມພາ	February
mîi-náa	ມີນາ	March
mée-săa	ເມສາ	April
put-sà-paa	ພຶດສະພາ	May
mì-tù-náa	ມິຖຸນາ	June
gɔɔ̀-la-gŏt	ກໍລະກົດ	July
sĭng-hăa	ສິງຫາ	August
gàn-ñáa	ກັນຍາ	September
dtù-láa	ຕຸລາ	October
pa-jĭk	ພະຈິກ	November
tán-wáa	ທັນວາ	December
mûu-nîi	ມື້ນີ້	today
mûu-wáan-nîi	ມື້ວານນີ້	yesterday

mûu-ʉʉn	ມື້ອື່ນ	tomorrow
tuk/tuk-tuk	ທຸກ/ທຸກໆ	every
sɔ̌ɔng mûu gɔɔn	ສອງມື້ກ່ອນ	two days ago
sǎam mûu gɔɔn	ສາມມື້ກ່ອນ	three days ago
ìik sɔ̌ɔng mûu	ອີກສອງມື້	two days from now
ìik sǎam mûu	ອີກສາມມື້	three days from now
tuk-tuk mûu	ທຸກໆມື້	everyday
àa-tit/sǎp-pa-dàa	ອາທິດ/ສັບປະດາ	week[1]
àa-tit-nîi	ອາທິດນີ້	this week
àa-tit gɔɔn/àa-tit-lɛ̂ɛo		last week
ອາທິດກ່ອນ/ອາທິດແລ້ວ		
àa-tit nàa	ອາທິດໜ້າ	next week
sɔ̌ɔng àa-tit gɔɔn		
ສອງອາທິດກ່ອນ		two weeks ago
sǎam àa-tit gɔɔn		
ສາມອາທິດກ່ອນ		three weeks ago
ìik sɔ̌ɔng àa-tit	ອີກສອງອາທິດ	two weeks from now
ìik sǎam àa-tit	ອີກສາມອາທິດ	three weeks from now
tuk-tuk àa-tit	ທຸກໆອາທິດ	every week
dʉan-nîi	ເດືອນນີ້	this month
dʉan-lɛ̂ɛo (nîi)	ເດືອນແລ້ວ (ນີ້)	last month
dʉan-nàa	ເດືອນໜ້າ	next month
sɔ̌ɔng dʉan gɔɔn		
ສອງເດືອນກ່ອນ		two months ago
sǎam dʉan gɔɔn		
ສາມເດືອນກ່ອນ		three months ago
ìik sɔ̌ɔng dʉan	ອີກສອງເດືອນ	two months from now

ìik sǎam dùan   ອີກສາມເດືອນ   three months from now

tuk-tuk dùan   ທຸກໆເດືອນ   every month

bpìi   ປີ   year

bpìi-nîi   ປີນີ້   this year

bpìi-gàai/bpìi lɛ̂ɛo (nîi)   ປີກາຍ/ປີແລ້ວ (ນີ້)   last year

bpìi-nàa   ປີໜ້າ   next year

sǒɔng bpìi gɔɔn   ສອງປີກ່ອນ   two years ago

ìik sǒɔng bpìi   ອີກສອງປີ   two years from now

tuk-tuk bpìi   ທຸກໆປີ   every year

dtɔ̀ɔn/mùu sâo   ຕອນ/ມື້ເຊົ້າ   morning

(mùu) sâo-nîi   (ມື້) ເຊົ້ານີ້   this morning

mùu-ùun sâo   ມື້ອື່ນເຊົ້າ   tomorrow morning

sâo-wán àa-tit   ເຊົ້າວັນອາທິດ   Sunday morning

tuk-tuk sâo   ທຸກໆເຊົ້າ   every morning

dtɔ̀ɔn/mùu lɛ́ɛng   ຕອນ/ມື້ແລງ   evening

mùu-lɛ́ɛng-nîi   ມື້ແລງນີ້   this evening

lɛ́ɛng-wáan-nîi   ແລງວານນີ້   yesterday evening

mùu-ùun-lɛ́ɛng   ມື້ອື່ນແລງ   tomorrow evening

lɛ́ɛng wán-àa-tit   ແລງວັນອາທິດ   Sunday evening

tuk-tuk lɛ́ɛng   ທຸກໆແລງ   every evening

(gàang) kúun   (ກາງ) ຄືນ   night

dtɔɔn-kam-mùu-nîi   ຕອນຄ່ຳມື້ນີ້   tonight

mùu-kúun-(wáan)-nîi   ມື້ຄືນ (ວານ) ນີ້   last night

kúun mùu-ùun   ຄືນມື້ອື່ນ   tomorrow night

kúun wán-àa-tit   ຄືນວັນອາທິດ   Sunday night

tuk-tuk kúun   ທຸກໆຄືນ   every night

kón hak ຄົນຮັກ	loved one
pʉan/muu ເພື່ອນ/ໝູ່	friend
pùu-baao ຜູ້ບ່າວ	boyfriend
pùu-sǎao ຜູ້ສາວ	girlfriend
waang ຫວ່າງ	to have free time
ñùng ຫຍຸ້ງ	busy
dtôŋ ຕ້ອງ	must
míi ມີ	to have, there is/are
bpǔk ປຸກ	to wake someone up
mʉ́a/gǎp/kʉ́ʉn ເມືອ/ກັບ/ຄືນ	to return
bpài-tiao ໄປທ່ຽວ	to take a trip[3]
máa-hap ມາຮັບ	to come to pick up
bpài-hap ໄປຮັບ	to go to pick up
dtɛɛ-sâo ແຕ່ເຊົ້າ	early morning
dǒk ດຶກ	late at night
gǎp/nám-gàn ກັບ/ນຳກັນ	and, together with
bpai nám-gàn ໄປນຳກັນ	to go together
kón-dìao/pùu-dìao ຄົນດຽວ/ຜູ້ດຽວ	by oneself
míi-nat ມີນັດ	have a date, appointment
pop-gàn-mai ພົບກັນໃໝ່	"see you again"
aa-lǒo ອັນໂຫລ	"hello" (on the phone)
òo-kée ໂອເຄ	O.K.

1. àa-tit (ອາທິດ) means "week." Don't get it mixed up with
   wán-àa-tit (ວັນອາທິດ) which means "Sunday."

2. máng-gɔ̀ɔn (ມັງກອນ) is sometimes seen written as mok-ga-láa (ມົກກະລາ) .

3. bpài-tiao (ໄປທ່ຽວ) means to take a pleasure trip or to simply go out
   for pleasure.

Conversation

Tim: aa-lŏo.

ທິມ: ອາໂຫລ

       Hello.

Jampa: aa-lŏo. nîi mɛɛn jàm-bpàa wâo.

ຈຳປາ: ອາໂຫລ. ນີ້ ແມ່ນ ຈຳປາ ເວົ້າ.

       Hello.   Jampa speaking.

Tim: sa-bàai-dìi jàm-bpàa. nîi mɛɛn tím nă.*

ທິມ: ສະບາຍດີ ຈຳປາ. ນີ້ ແມ່ນ ທິມ ນະ.

       Hi Jampa. It's Tim speaking.

Jampa: sabàai dìi tim. jao sa-bàai dìi bɔɔ.

ຈຳປາ: ສະບາຍ ດີ ທິມ. ເຈົ້າ ສະບາຍ ດີ ບໍ່?

       Hi Tim. How are you?

Tim: kɔì sa-bàai dìi. mûu-ʉʉn lɛɛng jâo waang bɔɔ.

ທິມ: ຂ້ອຍ ສະບາຍ ດີ. ມື້ອື່ນ ແລງ ເຈົ້າ ຫວ່າງ ບໍ່?

       I'm fine. Are you free tomorrow night?

Jampa: bɔɔ, kɔì bɔɔ waang. mûu-ʉʉn lɛɛng kɔì dtông het wîak.

ຈຳປາ: ບໍ່, ຂ້ອຍ ບໍ່ ຫວ່າງ. ມື້ອື່ນ ແລງ ຂ້ອຍ ຕ້ອງ ເຮັດ ວຽກ.

       No, I'm not. I have to work tomorrow night.

Tim: lɛɛo wán-sŭk dèe.

ທິມ: ແລ້ວ ວັນ ສຸກ ເດ?

       What about Friday?

Jampa: kʉʉn wán-sŭk waang yuu.*

ຈຳປາ: ຄືນ ວັນສຸກ ຫວ່າງ ຢູ່.

       I'm free Friday night.

Tim: kɔì ja bpài gìn àa-hăan ñii-bpun.

ທິມ: ຂ້ອຍ ຈະ ໄປ ກິນ ອາຫານ ຍີ່ປຸ່ນ.

       I will go eat at a Japanese restaurant.

("nă" and "yuu" is an ending particle used for emphasis.)

bpài nám-gàn bɔɔ.

ໄປ   ນຳກັນ   ບໍ?

Do you want to go with me?

Jampa: òo-kée. kúɯn wán-sǔk bpài dâi yuu.

ຈຳປາ: ໂອ ເຄ.   ຄືນ   ວັນສຸກ   ໄປ   ໄດ້ ຢູ່.

O.K. I can go Friday night.

jâo jǎ bpài jǎk móong.

ເຈົ້າ ຈະ ໄປ   ຈັກ ໂມງ?

What time are you going?

Tim: bpa-máan bpɛ̀ɛt móong.

ທິມ: ປະມານ   ແປດ   ໂມງ.

About eight o'clock.

kɔ̀i jǎ bpài-hap jâo dtɔ̀ɔn hǒk móong kəng dɔ́ə.

ຂ້ອຍ ຈະ ໄປຮັບ   ເຈົ້າ ຕອນ ຫົກ   ໂມງ ເຄິ່ງ ດຶ້.

("dɔ́ə" is an ending particle used for suggestion, persuasion or asking for

an agreement.)

I will go pick you up at half past six.

Jampa: kɔ̀ɔp-jai. lɛ̂ɛo pop gàn wán-sǔk dtɔ̀ɔn hǒk móong kəng.

ຈຳປາ: ຂອບໃຈ. ແລ້ວ ພົບ ກັນ ວັນສຸກ ຕອນ ຫົກ ໂມງ ເຄິ່ງ.

Thank you. See you Friday at half past six.

Tim: tɔɔ-nîi nɔ.

ທິມ: ທໍ່ນີ້   ເນາະ.

Good-bye. (On the phone. Literally means "That's it.")

Jampa: sôok-dìi dɔ̂ɔ.

ຈຳປາ: ໂຊກດີ ດຶ້.

Good-luck.

bpà-ñòok   ປະໂຫຍກ   **Sentences**

1. A: mûu-nîi mɛɛn wán ñǎng.

    ມື້ນີ້ ແມ່ນ ວັນ ຫຍັງ?

    What day is today?

    B: mûu-nîi mɛɛn wán-àa-tit.

    ມື້ນີ້ ແມ່ນ ວັນອາທິດ.

    Today is Sunday.

2. A: mûu-ʉʉn mɛɛn wán ñǎng.

    ມື້ອື່ນ ແມ່ນ ວັນ ຫຍັງ?

    What day is tomorrow?

    B: mûu-ʉʉn mɛɛn wán-jàn.

    ມື້ອື່ນ ແມ່ນ ວັນຈັນ.

    Tomorrow is Monday.

3. A: dʉan nîi mɛɛn dʉan ñǎng.

    ເດືອນ ນີ້ ແມ່ນ ເດືອນ ຫຍັງ?

    What month is this?

    B: dʉan nîi mɛɛn dʉan míi-náa.

    ເດືອນ ນີ້ ແມ່ນ ເດືອນ ມີນາ.

    This month is March.

4. A: bpìi nîi mɛɛn bpìi ñǎng.

    ປີ ນີ້ ແມ່ນ ປີ ຫຍັງ?

    What year is this?

    B: bpìi nîi mɛɛn bpìi sɔ́ɔng-pán-sǎam.

    ປີ ນີ້ ແມ່ນ ປີ ສອງພັນສາມ.

    This year is 2003.

5. A: mûu-nîi mɛɛn wán-tíi tao-dǎi.

    ມື້ນີ້ ແມ່ນ ວັນທີ ເທົ່າໃດ?

    What is the date today?

    B: mûu-nîi mɛɛn wán-tíi sǐp-hàa.

    ມື້ນີ້ ແມ່ນ ວັນທີ ສິບຫ້າ.

    Today is the 15th.

C: mùu-nîi mɛɛn wán-tîi sǐp-hàa dùan mée-sǎa.

ມື້ນີ້   ແມ່ນ   ວັນທີ   ສິບຫ້າ   ເດືອນ   ເມສາ.

Today is April 15th.

D: mùu-nîi mɛɛn wán-sǎo tîi sǐp-hàa dùan mée-sǎa.

ມື້ນີ້   ແມ່ນ   ວັນເສົາ   ທີ   ສິບຫ້າ   ເດືອນ   ເມສາ.

Today is Saturday, April 15th.

6.   A: jâo ja bpài múang láao dùan dǎi.

ເຈົ້າ ຈະ ໄປ   ເມືອງ   ລາວ   ເດືອນ ໃດ?

What month are you going to Laos?

B: kòi ja bpài múang láao dùan gàn-ñáa.

ຂ້ອຍ ຈະ ໄປ   ເມືອງ   ລາວ   ເດືອນ   ກັນຍາ.

I will go to Laos in September.

7.   A: jâo mîi wán-pak múa-dǎi.

ເຈົ້າ ມີ   ວັນພັກ   ເມື່ອໃດ?

When do you have a holiday?

B: kòi mîi wán-pak dùan nàa.

ຂ້ອຍ ມີ   ວັນພັກ   ເດືອນ ໜ້າ.

I have a holiday next month.

8.   A: wán-àa-tit nîi jâo jǎ het ñǎng.

ວັນອາທິດ   ນີ້ ເຈົ້າ ຈະ ເຮັດ ຫຍັງ?

What will you do this coming Sunday?

B: wán-àa-tit nîi kòi jǎ bpài gìn àa-hǎan láao.

ວັນອາທິດ   ນີ້ ຂ້ອຍ ຈະ ໄປ ກິນ ອາຫານ ລາວ.

This Sunday I will go to eat Lao food.

9.   A: mùu-kúun-wáan-nîi jâo het ñǎng.

ມື້ຄືນວານນີ້   ເຈົ້າ ເຮັດ ຫຍັງ?

What did you do last night?

B: kòi bpài gìn bìa gǎp muu.

ຂ້ອຍ ໄປ ກິນ ເບຍ ກັບ ໝູ່.

I went to drink beer with a friend.

10. A: láao yuu múang láao jăk bpìi.
    ລາວ ຢູ່ ເມືອງ ລາວ ຈັກ ປີ?
    How long was he in Laos?

   B: láao yuu múang láao hàa bpìi.
    ລາວ ຢູ່ ເມືອງ ລາວ ຫ້າ ປີ.
    He was in Laos for five years.

11. A: àa-tit nàa jâo jă het ñăng.
    ອາທິດ ໜ້າ ເຈົ້າ ຈະ ເຮັດ ຫຍັງ?
    What will you do next week?

   B: àa-tit nàa kɔ̀i jă bpai ñii-bpun.
    ອາທິດ ໜ້າ ຂ້ອຍ ຈະ ໄປ ຍີ່ປຸ່ນ.
    Next week I will go to Japan.

12. múu-wáan-nìi kɔ̀i lóm tóo-ra-săp kəng sua-móong.
    ມື້ວານນີ້ ຂ້ອຍ ລົມ ໂທລະສັບ ເຄິ່ງ ຊົ່ວໂມງ.
    Yesterday I talked on the phone for half an hour.

13. kɔ̀i hían páa-săa láao tuk àa-tit.
    ຂ້ອຍ ຮຽນ ພາສາ ລາວ ທຸກ ອາທິດ.
    I study Lao every week.

14. kɔ̀i hían páa-săa láao tuk wán-àa-tit.
    ຂ້ອຍ ຮຽນ ພາສາ ລາວ ທຸກ ວັນອາທິດ.
    I study Lao every Sunday.

15. láao máa het wîak dtɛɛ dǒk.
    ລາວ ມາ ເຮັດ ວຽກ ແຕ່ ເດິກ.
    He comes to work early in the morning.

16. săo-àa-tit kɔ̀i mak dtʉʉn sǔai.
    ເສົາອາທິດ ຂ້ອຍ ມັກ ຕື່ນ ສວຍ.
    I like to wake up late on weekends.

17. A: pûak-jâo yuu múang-láao jăk dùan.
    ພວກເຈົ້າ ຢູ່ ເມືອງລາວ ຈັກ ເດືອນ?
    How many months were you in Laos?

B: pûak-háo yuu mɯ̂ang-láao sǎam dɯ̀an.

ພວກເຮົາ   ຢູ່   ເມືອງລາວ   ສາມ   ເດືອນ

We were in Laos for three months.

18.   pûak-háo yuu mɯ̂ang-láao dtɛɛ dɯ̀an mi-tu-náa tǎng dɯ̀an sǐng hǎa.

ພວກເຮົາ   ຢູ່   ເມືອງລາວ   ແຕ່   ເດືອນ   ມິຖຸນາ   ເຖິງ   ເດືອນ   ສີງຫາ.

We were in Laos from June to August.

(The word "dɯ̀an" can be dropped in front of the month.)

19.   láao mîi wée-láa waang tuk sǎo-àa-tit.

ລາວ   ມີ   ເວລາ   ຫວ່າງ   ທຸກ   ເສົາອາທິດ.

He has free time every weekend.

20.   sɔ̌ɔng mɯ̂ɯ paan máa kɔ̀i bpài het wîak sǔai.

ສອງ   ມື້   ຜ່ານ   ມາ   ຂ້ອຍ   ໄປ   ເຣັດ   ວຽກ   ສວຍ.

The last two days I went to work late.

21.   bpɯ̀ii-nàa kɔ̀i jǎ hían páa-sǎa láao gǎp páa-sǎa jìin.

ປີ   ໜ້າ   ຂ້ອຍ   ຈະ   ຮຽນ   ພາສາ   ລາວ   ກັບ   ພາສາ   ຈິນ.

Next year I will study Lao and Chinese.

22.   àa-tit lɛ̂ɛo kɔ̀i mɯa-bâan dɔ̌k tuk mɯ̂ɯ.

ອາທິດ   ແລ້ວ   ຂ້ອຍ   ເມືອບ້ານ   ເດິກ   ທຸກ   ມື້.

Last week I returned home late everyday.

23.   ìik sǎam bpɯ̀ii kɔ̀i jǎ gǎp bpài mɯ̂ang láao.

ອີກ   ສາມ   ປີ   ຂ້ອຍ   ຈະ   ກັບ   ໄປ   ເມືອງ   ລາວ.

I will return to Laos in three years.

24.   mɯ̂ɯ sáo-nîi kɔ̀i gìn kâo kón dìao.

ມື້   ເຊົ້າ   ນີ້   ຂ້ອຍ   ກິນ   ເຂົ້າ   ຄົນ   ດຽວ.

This morning I ate breakfast by myself.

25.   kɔ̀i mîi-nat gǎp pùu-sǎao kɔ̀i tuk kɯ̀ɯn wán-sǔk.

ຂ້ອຍ   ມີ   ນັດ   ກັບ   ຜູ້   ສາວ   ຂ້ອຍ   ທຸກ   ຄືນ   ວັນ   ສຸກ.

I have a date with my girlfriend every Friday night.

Test 5

Match the English words with the Lao words.

<u>Days</u> ວັນ

_____ 1. Sunday   a. wán-pa-hăt ວັນພະຫັດ

_____ 2. Monday   b. wán-săo ວັນເສົາ

_____ 3. Tuesday   c. wán-àa-tit ວັນອາທິດ

_____ 4. Wednesday   d. wán-sŭk ວັນສຸກ

_____ 5. Thursday   e. wán-jàn ວັນຈັນ

_____ 6. Friday   f. wán-àng káan ວັນອັງຄານ

_____ 7. Saturday   g. wán-pak ວັນພັກ

_____ 8. holiday   h. wán-put ວັນພຸດ

Months ເດືອນ

_____ 1. January

_____ 2. February

_____ 3. March

_____ 4. April

_____ 5. May

_____ 6. June

_____ 7. July

_____ 8. August

_____ 9. September

_____ 10. October

_____ 11. November

_____ 12. December

a. mée-săa
   ເມສາ

b. tán-wáa
   ທັນວາ

c. sǐng-hǎa
   ສິງຫາ

d. pa-jik
   ພະຈິກ

e. gùm-páa
   ກຸມພາ

f. gàn-ñáa
   ກັນຍາ

g. put-sà-páa
   ພຶດສະພາ

h. mi-tù-náa
   ມິຖຸນາ

i. máng-gɔ̀ɔn
   ມັງກອນ

j. gɔ̀ɔ-la-gŏt
   ກໍລະກົດ

k. dtu-láa
   ຕຸລາ

l. mîi-náa
   ມີນາ

Tone Marks With High Consonants

With high consonant syllables, there are three possible tones and two tone marks which may be used.

Tone Mark	Tone Name	Tone	Examples
່	sĭang săa-mán	mid	ຂາ (kaa)
້	sĭang èek	low	ຂ່າ (kàa)

When there is no tone mark, a high consonant syllable has either rising tone or low tone depending on the combination of the vowel and the ending consonant. (See page 103-104)

Reading Exercise: Read the following words and practice writing them in Lao. Also identify the tones.

1. ສີ່ four

2. ຫໍ່ to wrap

3. ຂ້າວ rice

4. ສົ້ນ heel, end

5. ຂັ້ນ step, level

6. ຫັ່ນ to slice

7. ຜ້າ cloth

8. ໃຫ້ to give

9. ຝິ່ນ opium

10. ຖ້ຳ cave

11. ຫ້າມ to prohibit

12. ສົ້ມ sour

13. ຫ້າ five

14. ເຝົ້າ to watch over

Read The Following Aloud

1. ວ່າ   ວ້າ   ວາ   6. ສື່   ສື້   ສື

2. ຖຸ່   ຖຸ້   ຖຸ   7. ແຜ່   ແຜ້   ແຜ

3. ໄຜ່   ໄຜ້   ໄຜ   8. ເສົ່າ   ເສົ້າ   ເສົາ

4. ທ່ຳ   ທ້ຳ   ທຳ   9. ໂວ່   ໂວ້   ໂວ

5. ແສ່   ແສ້   ແສ   10. ຕຶ່   ຕຶ້   ຕຶ

Writing Exercise 5

Transcribe the following into Lao script.

1. sɔi _____   11. sǔai _____

2. pùng _____   12. fang _____

3. hùan _____   13. tii _____

4. kǒm _____   14. faan _____

5. pʉʉn _____   15. kǎai _____

6. tɔɔi _____   16. kào _____

7. song _____   17. hɔ̀ng _____

8. kùut _____   18. fàai _____

9. pɔ̌ɔi _____   19. sàap _____

10. tǎam _____   20. sèn _____

Low Consonants
ອັກສອນຕ່ຳ (ǎk-sɔ̌ɔn-dtam)

There are twelve "low" consonants in Lao. You have seen five of them before as sonorant finals (ງ, ນ, ມ, ຍ, ວ) .

Consonant		Consonant Name	Sound
ຄ	ຄ ຄວາຍ	kɔ́ɔ kwáai - buffalo	/k/
ງ	ງ ງົວ	ngɔ́ɔ ngúa - cow	/ng/
ຊ	ຊ ຊ້າງ	sɔ́ɔ sâang - elephant	/s/
ຍ	ຍ ຍຸງ	ñɔ́ɔ nyúng - mosquito	/ñ/
ທ	ທ ທຸງ	tɔ́ɔ túng - flag	/t/
ນ	ນ ນົກ	nɔ́ɔ nok - bird	/n/
ພ	ພ ພູ	pɔ́ɔ púu - mountain	/p/
ຟ	ຟ ໄຟ	fɔ́ɔ fái - fire	/f/
ມ	ມ ແມວ	mɔ́ɔ mέεo - cat	/m/
ລ	ລ ລິງ	lɔ́ɔ líng - monkey	/l/
ວ	ວ ວີ	wɔ́ɔ wíi - fan	/w/
ຣ	ຣ ເຮືອນ	hɔ́ɔ húan - house	/h/

Lesson 6

'ào' (to get), 'yàak' (to want); 'gàm-láng' (to be ... ing); tone rules for low consonants

bŏt-tíi hŏk   ບົດທີ ຫົກ   Lesson 6

kám-săp   ຄຳສັບ   Vocabulary

gàm-láng	ກຳລັງ	to be ...ing
gàm-láng jă	ກຳລັງຈະ	to be going to
bɔɔ kɔi .../bpaan-dăi	ບໍ່ຄ່ອຍ..../ ປານໃດ	not so ...
bɔɔ ... lə́əi	ບໍ່ .... ເລີຍ	not ... at all
jang-dăi/yaang-dăi	ຈັ່ງໃດ/ ຢ່າງໃດ	how
yàak	ຢາກ	to want to do something
ào	ເອົາ	to get, take
kə́əi	ເຄີຍ	ever, used to
bpŏk-ga-dĭ	ປົກກະຕິ	normally
bpa-jàm	ປະຈຳ	usually, regularly
lɯ̂ai-lɯ̂ai	ເລື້ອຍໆ	often, frequently
ñáng/tɯa	ຍັງ/ເທື່ອ	yet, still
ñáng bɔɔ tán dâi ___ tɯa		not ___ yet
ບໍ່ຍັງບໍ່ທັນໄດ້ ___ ເທື່ອ		
lɛ̂ɛo/lɛ̂ɛo-lɛ̂ɛo	ແລ້ວ/ແລ້ວໆ	already
dìi	ດີ	good
fáng	ຟັງ	to listen
wâo/lóm	ເວົ້າ/ລົມ	to chat, talk
pop/pɔ̂ɔ	ພົບ/ ພໍ້	to meet, find
nang	ນັ່ງ	to sit
yɯɯn	ຢືນ	to stand
ñaang	ຍ່າງ	to walk
lɛɛn	ແລ່ນ	to run
sɯ́ɯ	ຊື້	to buy
kăai	ຂາຍ	to sell

hɔ̂ɔng ຮ້ອງ	to sing, cry out
dtên ເຕັ້ນ	to dance
fɔ̂ɔn/dtên-lám ຟ້ອນ/ເຕັ້ນລຳ	to dance (traditional)
lìn ຫຼິ້ນ	to play
bpài-hǎa ໄປຫາ	to go to see someone
máa-hǎa ມາຫາ	to come to see someone
kǎp ຂັບ	to drive
kii ຂີ່	to ride
dtǒk/lon/lôm ຕົກ/ຫຼົ່ນ/ລົ້ມ	to fall
wîak ວຽກ	work
tu-la/wîak ທຸລະ/ວຽກ	errand
péeng ເພງ	song
dòoi ໂດຍ	by
lot ລົດ	vehicle, car
lot-fái ລົດໄຟ	train
lot-fái-dtâi-dìn ລົດໄຟໃຕ້ດິນ	subway
lot-mée ລົດເມ	bus
dtak-sîi/tɛk-sîi ຕັກຊີ້/ແທກຊີ້	taxi
lot-sɔ̂ɔng-tɛ̌ɛo ລົດສອງແຖວ	minibus
lot-sǎam-lɔ̂ɔ ລົດສາມລໍ້	tricycle
lot-dtuk-dtuk ລົດຕຸກໆ	tricycle taxi
lot-jǎk ລົດຈັກ	motorcycle
lot-tìip ລົດຖີບ	bicycle
húa-bìn/yón ເຮືອບິນ/ຍົນ	airplane
húa ເຮືອ	boat, ship
fǒn ຝົນ	rain
hi-ma ຫິມະ	snow
dtôn-mâi ຕົ້ນໄມ້	tree
púu ພູ	mountain
ta-lée ທະເລ	sea

mɛɛ-nâm	ແມ່ນ້ຳ	river
dìn	ດິນ	soil
lóm	ລົມ	wind
fái	ໄຟ	fire
hâan-lám-wóng	ຮ້ານລຳວົງ	disco
káa-láa-òo-gě	ຄາລາໂອເກະ	karaoke
kɔ̌ɔ-wâo gǎp	ຂໍເວົ້າກັບ	"May I speak with ...?"

Conversation

Somsuk: aa-lŏo. kɔ̌ɔ wâo gàp juu-ĺii dɛɛ.

ສົມສຸກ: ອາໂຫຼ. ຂໍ ເວົ້າ ກັບ ຈູລີ ແດ່?

Hello! May I speak with Julie?

Julie: gàm-láng wâo yuu.

ຈູລີ:   ກຳລັງ ເວົ້າ ຢູ່.

Speaking.

Somsuk: jâo gàm-láng het ñăng yuu.

ສົມສຸກ: ເຈົ້າ ກຳລັງ ເຮັດ ຫຍັງ ຢູ່?

What are you doing Julie?

Julie: kòi gàm-láng gìn kào. jâo gìn kâo lɛ̂ɛo bɔɔ.

ຈູລີ:   ຂ້ອຍ ກຳລັງ ກິນ ເຂົ້າ. ເຈົ້າ ກິນ ເຂົ້າ ແລ້ວ ບໍ່?

I'm going to eat. Have you eaten?

Somsuk: gìn lêɛo la.

ສົມສຸກ: ກິນ ແລ້ວ ລະ.

Yes, I have.

            mɯ̂ɯ-nîi kɔ̀i yàak bpài lìn káa-láa-òo-gĕ.

            ມື້ນີ້ ຂ້ອຍ ຢາກ ໄປ ຫຼິ້ນ ຄາລາໂອເກະ,

            I'm going to Karaoke today.

            jâo ja bpai nám kòi bɔɔ.

            ເຈົ້າ ຈະ ໄປ ນຳ ຂ້ອຍ ບໍ່?

            Do you want to go with me today?

Julie: bpài. kòi ñáng bɔɔ tán kɔ̀əi bpài jăk tɯa.

ຈູລີ :   ໄປ. ຂ້ອຍ ຍັງ ບໍ່ ທັນ ເຄີຍ ໄປ ຈັກ ເທື່ອ.

Yes. I've never been to one yet.

bpà-ñòok   ປະໂຫຍກ   Sentences

1. A: pûak-jâo gàm-láng het ñăng.
      ພວກເຈົ້າ   ກຳລັງ   ເຮັດ ຫຍັງ?
      What are you doing?

    B: pûak-háo gàm-láng gìn kào.
      ພວກເຮົາ   ກຳລັງ   ກິນ ເຂົ້າ.
      We are eating.

    C: pûak-jâo gàm-láng jǎ het ñăng.
      ພວກເຈົ້າ   ກຳລັງ   ຈະ ເຮັດ ຫຍັງ?
      What are you going to do?

    D: pûak-háo gàm-láng jǎ bəng tóo-la-tat.
      ພວກເຮົາ   ກຳລັງ   ຈະ ເບິ່ງ ໂທລະຫັດ.
      We are going to watch TV.

2. A: jâo gìn kào lɛ̂ɛo bɔɔ.
      ເຈົ້າ ກິນ ເຂົ້າ ແລ້ວ ບໍ່?
      Have you eaten?

    B: gìn lɛ̂ɛo.
      ກິນ ແລ້ວ.
      Yes, I have.

    C: ñǎng bɔɔ tán dâi gìn tɯa.
      ຍັງ   ບໍ່ ທັນ ໄດ້ ກິນ ເຖື່ອ.
      No, I haven't.

    D: jâo bəng tóo-la-tat lɛ̂ɛo bɔɔ.
      ເຈົ້າ ເບິ່ງ   ໂທລະຫັດ ແລ້ວ ບໍ່?
      Have you watched TV?

    E: bəng lɛ̂ɛo-lɛ̂ɛo.
      ເບິ່ງ   ແລ້ວໆ.
      Yes, I have.

F: ñáng, ñáng bɔɔ dâi bəng tɯa.

ບໍ່,   ບໍ່   ບໍ່   ໄດ້ ເບິ່ງ ເທື່ອ.

No, I haven't.

3. A: jâo yàak (jǎ) het ñǎng.

ເຈົ້າ ຢາກ (ຈະ) ເຮັດ ຫຍັງ?

What do you want to do?

B: kɔ̀i yàak (jǎ) gìn kào.

ຂ້ອຍ ຢາກ (ຈະ) ກິນ ເຂົ້າ.

I want to eat.

C: kɔ̀i yàak (jǎ) bəng tóo-la-tat.

ຂ້ອຍ ຢາກ (ຈະ) ເບິ່ງ ໂທລະທັດ.

I want to watch TV.

4. A: jâo kə́əi dâi bpài múang láao bɔɔ.

ເຈົ້າ ເຄີຍ ໄດ້ ໄປ ເມືອງ ລາວ ບໍ່?

Have you ever been to Laos?

B: kə́əi.

ເຄີຍ.

Yes, I have.

C: bɔɔ kə́əi.

ບໍ່ ເຄີຍ

No, I haven't.

D: jâo kə́əi kii lot dtuk-dtuk lɛ̂ɛo bɔɔ.

ເຈົ້າ ເຄີຍ ຂີ່ ລົດ ຕຸກໆ   ແລ້ວ ບໍ່?

Have you ever ridden in a tricycle taxi?

E: kə́əi kii lɛ̂ɛo.

ເຄີຍ ຂີ່ ແລ້ວ.

Yes, I already have.

F: ñáng, ñáng bɔɔ kə́əi kii.

ບໍ່,   ບໍ່   ບໍ່   ເຄີຍ ຂີ່.

No, I haven't.

5. A: àn nĭi bɔɔ kɔi dìi.
        ອັນ ນີ້ ບໍ່ ຄ່ອຍ ດີ.
        This one is not very good.

    B: kɔ̀i bɔɔ kɔi mak àa-hăan fa-lang.
        ຂ້ອຍ ບໍ່ ຄ່ອຍ ມັກ ອາຫານ ຝຣັ່ງ.
        I don't like foreign food very much.

    C: taan kám-pán bɔɔ kɔi mĭi ngə́n lăai bpàan-dăi.
        ທ່ານ ຄຳພັນ ບໍ່ ຄ່ອຍ ມີ ເງິນ ຫລາຍ ປານໃດ.
        Mr. Kampan does not have very much money.

6. A: àn-nĭi bɔɔ kɔi dìi bpàan-dăi.
        ອັນນີ້ ບໍ່ ຄ່ອຍ ດີ ປານໃດ.
        This one is not good at all.

    B: kɔ̀i bɔɔ kɔi mak àa-hăan fa-làng bpàan-dăi.
        ຂ້ອຍ ບໍ່ ຄ່ອຍ ມັກ ອາຫານ ຝຣັ່ງ ປານໃດ.
        I don't like western food at all.

    C: taan kám-pán bɔɔ mĭi ngə́n jăk-nɔ̀i lə́əi.
        ທ່ານ ຄຳພັນ ບໍ່ ມີ ເງິນ ຈັກຫນ້ອຍ ເລີຍ.
        Mr. Kampan does not have any money at all.

7. A: taan kám-pán bpài gìn àa-hăan láao bpa-jàm.
        ທ່ານ ຄຳພັນ ໄປ ກິນ ອາຫານ ລາວ ປະຈຳ.
        Mr. Kampan goes to eat Lao food regularly.

    B: taan kám-pán bpài gìn àa-hăan láao lûai lûai.
        ທ່ານ ຄຳພັນ ໄປ ກິນ ອາຫານ ລາວ ເລື້ອຍໆ.
        Mr. Kampan goes to eat Laos food often.

    C: taan kám-pán bpài gìn àa-hăan láao tuk wán-put.
        ທ່ານ ຄຳພັນ ໄປ ກິນ ອາຫານ ລາວ ທຸກ ວັນພຸດ.
        Mr. Kampan goes to eat Lao food every Wednesday.

8. A: bpŏk-ga-dtĭ jâo bpài het wîak jang dăi.
        ປົກກະຕີ ເຈົ້າ ໄປ ເຮັດ ວຽກ ຈັ່ງ ໃດ?
        How do you normally go to work?

B: kǎp lot bpài.

ຂັບ ລົດ ໄປ.

I drive.

C: nang dtak-sîi bpài.

ນັ່ງ ຕັກຊີ້ ໄປ.

I take a taxi.

D: kii lot jǎk bpài.

ຂີ້ ລົດ ຈັກ ໄປ.

I ride a motorcycle.

E: ñaang bpài.

ຍ່າງ ໄປ.

I walk.

9. A: jâo bpài sǎi máa.

ເຈົ້າ ໄປ ໃສ ມາ?

Where have you been?

B: kòi bpài gìn kào máa.

ຂ້ອຍ ໄປ ກິນ ເຂົ້າ ມາ.

I went to eat.

C: jâo sʉ̂ʉ ñǎng (máa).

ເຈົ້າ ຊື້ ຫຍັງ (ມາ)?

What did you buy?

D: kòi sʉ̂ʉ kà-nǒm (máa).

ຂ້ອຍ ຊື້ ຂະໜົມ (ມາ).

I bought snacks.

máa (ມາ) at the end of these sentences literally means to have
done something and come back, which implies the past tense.

10. A: kòi yàak bpài hǎa jâo.

ຂ້ອຍ ຢາກ ໄປ ຫາ ເຈົ້າ.

I want to go to see you.

B: mûu-wáan-nîi láao máa hǎa kɔ̀i.

ມື້ ວານ ນີ້ ລາວ ມາ ຫາ ຂ້ອຍ.

Yesterday he came to see me.

C: láao tóo-la-sǎp máa-hǎa jâo.

ລາວ ໂທລະສັບ ມາຫາ ເຈົ້າ.

He gave you a call.

D: kɔ̀i ñaang bpài-hǎa láao.

ຂ້ອຍ ຍ່າງ ໄປຫາ ລາວ.

I walk to (meet) him.

11.   fǒn (gàm-láng) dtǒk.

ຝົນ (ກຳລັງ) ຕົກ.

It's raining.

12.   kɔ̀i kii lot bpài het wîak.

ຂ້ອຍ ຂີ່ ລົດ ໄປ ເຮັດ ວຽກ.

I go to work by car.

13.   kɔ̀i mak lóm nám kón láao.

ຂ້ອຍ ມັກ ລົມ ນຳ ຄົນ ລາວ.

We like to talk to Lao people.

14.   yuu múang láao bɔɔ mîi hi-ma.

ຢູ່ ເມືອງ ລາວ ບໍ່ ມີ ຫິມະ.

There is no snow in Laos.

15.   yuu tɔng púu bɔɔ kɔi mîi dtôn-mâi.

ຢູ່ ເທິງ ພູ ບໍ່ ຄ່ອຍ ມີ ຕົ້ນໄມ້.

There are not so many trees in the mountains.

16.   bɔɔ mîi kón yuu húan lɔ̀əi.

ບໍ່ ມີ ຄົນ ຢູ່ ເຮືອນ ເລີຍ.

There isn't anybody at home at all.

17.   mûu-nîi kɔ̀i mîi wîak lǎai, kɔ̀i bpài-hǎa jâo bɔɔ dâi dɔ̀ɔk.

ມື້ນີ້ ຂ້ອຍ ມີ ວຽກ ຫລາຍ. ຂ້ອຍ ໄປຫາ ເຈົ້າ ບໍ່ ໄດ້ ດອກ.

Today, I have a lot of errands. I can't go to see you.

18. kɔ̀i gìn kào lɛ̂ɛo.
     ຂ້ອຍ ກິນ ເຂົ້າ ແລ້ວ.
     I already ate.

19. kɔ̀i ñáng bɔɔ dâi gìn kào tɯa.
     ຂ້ອຍ ຍັງ ບໍ່ ໄດ້ ກິນ ເຂົ້າ ເທື່ອ.
     I haven't eaten yet.

20. pûak-háo fáng péeng.
     ພວກເຮົາ ຟັງ ເພງ.
     We listened to music.

21. láao lóm gǎp jâo.
     ລາວ ລົມ ກັບ ເຈົ້າ.
     He talked to you.

22. kɔ̀i mak aan nǎng-sɯ̌ɯ yuu hɯ́an.
     ຂ້ອຍ ມັກ ອ່ານ ໜັງສື ຢູ່ ເຮືອນ.
     I like to read at home.

23. mɯ̂ɯ ɯɯn kɔ̀i yàak bpài tiao gǎp pùu-sǎao kɔ̌ɔng kɔ̀i.
     ມື້ ອື່ນ ຂ້ອຍ ຢາກ ໄປ ທ່ຽວ ກັບ ຜູ້ສາວ ຂອງ ຂ້ອຍ.
     Tomorrow I want to go out with my girlfriend.

24. dtɔ̀ɔn-nîi láao ñáng bɔɔ yàak hían páa-sǎa-láao tɯa.
     ຕອນນີ້ ລາວ ຍັງ ບໍ່ ຢາກ ຮຽນ ພາສາລາວ ເທື່ອ.
     He doesn't want to study Lao at the moment.

25. mɯ̂ɯ-nîi kɔ̀i bɔɔ yàak het ñǎng.
     ມື້ນີ້ ຂ້ອຍ ບໍ່ ຢາກ ເຮັດ ຫຍັງ.
     Today I don't want to do anything.

Test 6

Match the English verbs with the Lao verbs.

_____ 1. to talk/chat   a. fǎng ຟັງ

_____ 2. to listen   b. lɛɛn ແລ່ນ

_____ 3. to take a trip   c. dtŏk ຕົກ

_____ 4. to play   d. hɔ̂ɔng ຮ້ອງ

_____ 5. to wake up   e. ñaang ຍ່າງ

_____ 6. to drive   f. lɛ̂ɛo ແລ້ວ

_____ 7. to sit   g. yɯ̀ɯn ຢືນ

_____ 8. to run   h. bpài-tiao ໄປທ່ຽວ

_____ 9. to walk   i. lìn ຫລິ້ນ

_____ 10. to buy   j. aan ອ່ານ

_____ 11. to sell   k. sɯ̂ɯ ຊື້

_____ 12. to sing   l. dtɯɯn ຕື່ນ

_____ 13. to fall   m. yàak ຢາກ

_____ 14. to want to   n. nang ນັ່ງ

_____ 15. to stand   o. lóm ລົ້ມ

   p. kǎp ຂັບ

   q. kǎai ຂາຍ

Translate the following into English.

1. dtɔɔn-nîi kɔ̀i gàm-láng jǎ bpài dən-bìn.
    ຕອນນີ້   ຂ້ອຍ   ກຳລັງ   ຈະ   ໄປ   ເດີ່ນບິນ.

    _____

2. bpǒk-ga-dtǐ taan kám-pán kii lot-fái bpài het wîak.
    ປົກກະຕິ   ທ່ານ   ຄຳພັນ   ຂີ່   ລົດໄຟ   ໄປ   ເຮັດ   ວຽກ.

    _____

3. pûak-háo yàak míi hâan-àa-hǎan láao yuu àa-mée-li-gàa.
    ພວກ-ເຮົາ   ຢາກ   ມີ   ຮ້ານອາຫານ   ລາວ   ຢູ່   ອາເມລິກາ.

    _____

4. láao yuu mûang tái dtâng-dtɛɛ dùan mi-tu-náa.
    ລາວ   ຢູ່   ເມືອງ   ໄທ   ຕັ້ງແຕ່   ເດືອນ   ມິຖຸນາ.

    _____

5. kɔ̀i bɔɔ mak fáng péeng.
    ຂ້ອຍ   ບໍ່   ມັກ   ຟັງ   ເພງ.

    _____

Practice Writing the Low Consonants

There are 12 "low" consonants in Lao. We have already practiced five letters in the final consonants section in Lesson 3. Here are all of them again. Start near the ❶.

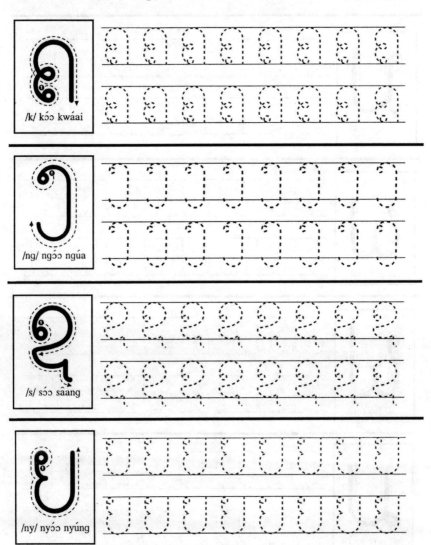

 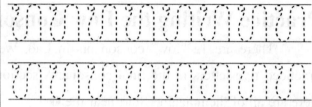

/t/ tɔɔ túng

 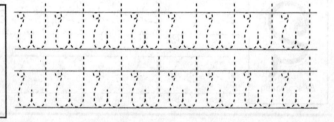

/n/ nɔɔ nok

 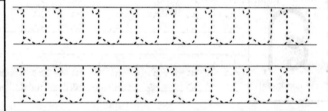

/p/ pɔɔ púu

 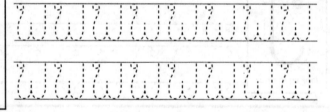

/f/ fɔɔ faǐ

 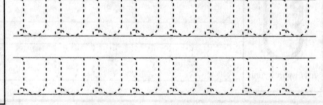

/m/ mɔɔ mɛ́ɛɔ

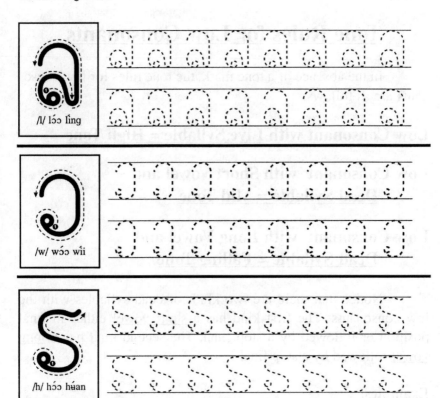

/l/ lóɔ líng

/w/ wóɔ wíi

/h/ hɔ́ɔ hǔan

<u>Tone Rules for Low Consonants</u>

In the absence of a tone mark, the tone rules for low consonants are as follows:

Low Consonant with <u>Live Syllable = High Tone</u>

Low Consonant with Short Vowel and <u>Dead Syllable = Mid Tone</u>

Low Consonant with Long Vowel and <u>Dead Syllable = Falling Tone</u>

Notice that there are two kinds of dead syllables with the
low consonants. The first kind has a <u>short vowel</u> either in final
position or followed by a stop final. The second kind has a <u>long
vowel</u> followed by a stop final.

Examples:

Low Consonant + Long Vowel = High Tone

	Sound Produced	Meaning
ม + –า	= มา (máa)	come
ฟ + ไ–	= ไฟ (fái)	fire
ม + ◌ื	= มื (múu)	hand

Exercise: Read the following words and practice writing them in Lao.

1. ເມຍ wife

2. ວິ fan

3. ພໍ enough

4. ໄພ fire

5. ລາ to say good-bye

6. ເນີຍ cheese

7. ເຮືອ ship

8. ນາຍ boss

9. ເມົາ drunk

10. ງາ sesame

11. ໃນ in

12. ເອົາ to take

13. ເຮົາ we

14. ທີ suffix for ordinal numbers e.g. 1st, 2nd

Writing Exercise 6

Transcribe the following into Lao script.

1. páa _____   11. tîi _____

2. sóo _____   12. ñɔ́ɔ _____

3. hám _____   13. fúu _____

4. múu _____   14. tée _____

5. sía _____   15. kɔ́ɔ _____

6. lía _____   16. kɨ̵ɨ̵ _____

7. sə́əi _____   17. ngáa _____

8. túa _____   18. péɛ _____

9. hɨ́a _____   19. ñám _____

10. fáo _____   20. lə́əi _____

Lesson 7

'dâi-ñín' (to hear); 'jɨɨ' (to remember);
'nɔ́ɔn-lǎp' (to fall asleep); 'bəng' (to look);
tone rules for low consonants (cont.)

bŏt-tíi jĕt ບົດທີ ເຈັດ Lesson 7

kám-săp ຄຳສັບ Vocabulary

păi ໃผ		who
kɔ̆ɔng ຂອງ		of
kɔ̆ɔng păi ຂອງໃผ		whose
dâi ໄດ້		can, okay
bɔɔ dâi ບໍ່ໄດ້ (after a verb)		cannot, not okay
bɔɔ dâi ບໍ່ໄດ້ (before a verb)		did not
lɔ́ɔi-nâam ລອຍນ້ຳ		to swim
juu/jàm ຈຳ		to memorize
juu dâi ຈຳໄດ້		to remember
juu bɔɔ dâi ຈຳບໍ່ໄດ້		can't remember
(jâo) juu dâi bɔɔ (ເຈົ້າ) ຈຳໄດ້ບໍ່?		Do you remember?
ñín/dâi-ñín/hûu-ñín ຍິນ/ໄດ້ຍິນ/ຮູ້ຍິນ		to hear, can hear
bɔɔ dâi-ñín ບໍ່ໄດ້ຍິນ		can't hear
(jâo) dâi-ñín bɔɔ (ເຈົ້າ) ໄດ້ຍິນບໍ່		Can you hear?
bəng ເບິ່ງ		to look
hĕn/bəng-hĕn ເຫັນ/ເບິ່ງເຫັນ		to see, can see
(bəng) bɔɔ hĕn (ເບິ່ງ) ບໍ່ເຫັນ		can't see
jâo (bəng) hĕn bɔɔ ເຈົ້າ (ເບິ່ງ) ເຫັນບໍ່?		Can you see?
hûu/sâap/hûu-jăk ຮູ້/ຊາບ/ຮູ້ຈັກ		to know[1]
nɔ́ɔn-lăp ນອນຫຼັບ		to fall asleep
nɔ́ɔn bɔɔ lăp ນອນບໍ່ຫຼັບ		can't fall asleep
lɛ́ɛo/săm-lĕt ແລ້ວ/ສຳເລັດ		to finish
ngăo-nɔ́ɔn ເຫງົານອນ		sleepy
dàng/sĭang-dàng ດັງ/ສຽງດັງ		loud

nùak-hǔu ໜວກຫູ | bothered by loud noise

(ǐt) mʉai (ອິດ) ເມື່ອຍ | tired

tán (wée-láa) ທັນ (ເວລາ) | on time, to keep up with

ɔ̀ɔk ອອກ | out

kit ຄິດ | to think

kit-hɔ̂ɔt ຄິດຮອດ | to think about, miss

kit waa ຄິດວ່າ | to think that ...

ñáam-dǎi/mʉa-dǎi ຍາມໃດ/ເມື່ອໃດ | When?

sâa/sâa-sâa ຊ້າ/ຊ້າໆ | slow/slowly

wái/wái-wái ໄວ/ໄວໆ | quick/quickly

tʉ̀ʉk ຖຶກ | correct

pǐt ຜິດ | incorrect

tɛ̂ɛ/jìng/ii-lǐi ແທ້/ຈິງ/ອີ່ຫລີ | true, really

sɛ̂ɛp ແຊບ | delicious

wǎan ຫວານ | sweet

kém ເຄັມ | salty

jʉ̀ʉt ຈຶດ | tasteless

sòm ສົ້ມ | sour

pět ເຜັດ | spicy, hot

---

1. sâap "to know" is a polite form of hǔu. Both sâap and
    hǔu are used without an object. hǔu-jǎk can be used
    with or without an object.
    e.g. kɔ̀i bɔɔ hǔu. *or* kɔ̀i bɔɔ sâap. = I don't know.
    kɔ̀i bɔɔ hǔu-jǎk láao. = I don't know him.

Conversation

Jane: sɔ̌ɔn, hʉan jâo yuu-sai.

ເຈນ: ສອນ, ເຮືອນ ເຈົ້າ ຢູ່ໃສ?

Where is your house, Sorn?

Sorn: yuu lʉ̌ang-pa-bàang. jâo hûu bɔɔ waa mán yuu sǎi.

ສອນ: ຢູ່ ຫລວງພະບາງ. ເຈົ້າ ຮູ້ ບໍ່ ວ່າ ມັນ ຢູ່ ໃສ?

In Luang Phrabang. Do you know where that is?

Jane: hûu. kɔ̀i hûu-jǎk

ເຈນ: ຮູ້. ອ້ອຍ ຮູ້ຈັກ.

Yes, I do.

Sorn: jâo máa mʉang láao dâi jǎk bpìi lέεo.

ສອນ: ເຈົ້າ ມາ ເມືອງ ລາວ ໄດ້ ຈັກ ປີ ແລ້ວ?

When did you come to Laos?

Jane: bpa-máan sǎam bpìi lέεo.

ເຈນ: ປະມານ ສາມ ປີ ແລ້ວ.

About three years ago.

Sorn: jâo mak àa-hǎan láao bɔɔ.

ສອນ: ເຈົ້າ ມັກ ອາຫານ ລາວ ບໍ່?

Do you like Lao food?

Jane: mak. àa-hǎan láao sέεp lǎai. kɔ̀i mak gìn pět.

ເຈນ: ມັກ. ອາຫານ ລາວ ແຊບ ຫລາຍ. ອ້ອຍ ມັກ ກິນ ເຜັດ.

Yes. Lao food is very good. I like spicy food.

Sorn: jâo aan páa-sǎa láao dâi bɔɔ.

ສອນ: ເຈົ້າ ອ່ານ ພາສາ ລາວ ໄດ້ ບໍ່?

Can you read Lao?

Jane: aan dâi nɔ̀i-nʉng. dtεε kǐan bɔɔ dâi.

ເຈນ: ອ່ານ ໄດ້ ໜ້ອຍນຶ່ງ. ແຕ່ ຂຽນ ບໍ່ ໄດ້.

I can read a little, but I can't write.

Son: jâo fáng tán bɔɔ.

ສອນ: ເຈົ້າ ຟັງ ທັນ ບໍ?

Can you understand (spoken Lao)?

(Literally: Can you catch up with listening?)

Jane: tàa wâo sâa-sâa, gɔɔ fáng tán yuu.

ເຈນ: ຖ້າ ເວົ້າ ຊ້າງ,   ກໍ   ຟັງ   ທັນ ຢູ່.

If (you) speak slowly, I can understand.

tàa wâo wái lǎai, gɔɔ fáng bɔɔ kɔi tán.

ຖ້າ ເວົ້າ ໄວ ຫລາຍ ກໍ   ຟັງ   ບໍ ຄ່ອຍ ທັນ.

If (you) speak fast, I don't understand very well.

bpà-ñòok   ປະໂຫຍກ   Sentences

1. A: nîi mɛn pǎi.

    ນີ້ ແມ່ນ ໃຜ?

    Who is this?

    B: nîi mɛn (taan) kám-pán.

    ນີ້ ແມ່ນ (ທ່ານ) ຄຳພັນ.

    This is Mr. Kampan.

2. A: nîi kɔ̌ɔng pǎi.

    ນີ້ ຂອງ ໃຜ?

    Whose is this?

    B: nîi kɔ̌ɔng kɔi.

    ນີ້ ຂອງ ຂ້ອຍ.

    This is mine.

    A: nîi mɛɛn hủan (kɔ̌ɔng)* pǎi.

    ນີ້ ແມ່ນ ເຮືອນ (ຂອງ)   ໃຜ?

    Whose house is this?

    B: nîi mɛɛn hủan (kɔ̌ɔng) kɔi.

    ນີ້ ແມ່ນ ເຮືອນ (ຂອງ)   ຂ້ອຍ.

    This is my house.

    * kɔ̌ɔng can be omitted when used with noun.

3. A: jâo lɔ́ɔi-nâam bpèn bɔɔ.
    ເຈົ້າ ລອຍນ້ຳ ເປັນ ບໍ່?
    Can you swim?

    B: lɔ́ɔi bpèn yuu.
    ລອຍ ເປັນ ຢູ່.
    Yes, I can.

    C: lɔ́ɔi bɔɔ bpèn.
    ລອຍ ບໍ່ ເປັນ.
    No, I can't.

4. A: juu kɔ̀i dâi bɔɔ.
    ຈື່ ຂ້ອຍ ໄດ້ ບໍ່?
    Do you remember me?

    B: juu dâi yuu.
    ຈື່ ໄດ້ ຢູ່.
    Yes, I do.

    C: juu bɔɔ dâi.
    ຈື່ ບໍ່ ໄດ້.
    No, I don't.

5. A: dâi-ñín bɔɔ.
    ໄດ້ຍິນ ບໍ່?
    Can you hear?

    B: dâi-ñín.
    ໄດ້ຍິນ.
    Yes, I can.

    C: bɔɔ dâi-ñín.
    ບໍ່ ໄດ້ຍິນ.
    No, I can't.

6. A: hěn láao bɔɔ.
    ເຫັນ ລາວ ບໍ່?
    Can you see him?

    B: hěn.
    ເຫັນ.
    Yes, I can.

Lesson 7

C: bɔɔ hěn.

ບໍ່ ເຫັນ.

No, I can't.

7. A: hûu-jǎk láao bɔɔ.

ຮູ້ຈັກ ລາວ ບໍ່?

Do you know him?

B: hûu-jǎk.

ຮູ້ຈັກ

Yes, I do.

C: bɔɔ, bɔɔ hûu-jǎk.

ບໍ່, ບໍ່ ຮູ້ຈັກ.

No, I don't.

8. A: lɛ̂ɛo lɛ̂ɛo bɔɔ.*

ແລ້ວ ແລ້ວ ບໍ່?

Are you ready?/Have you finished?

B: lɛ̂ɛo lɛ̂ɛo.*

ແລ້ວ ແລ້ວ.

Yes, I am./Yes, I have.

* The first lɛ̂ɛo means "to finish" or to "to get done" and the second one means "already."

C: ñáng bɔɔ lɛ̂ɛo.

ຍັງ ບໍ່ ແລ້ວ.

No, I'm not./No, I haven't.

9. mûu-kúun-nîi kɔ̀i nɔɔn bɔɔ kɔi lǎp.

ມື້ຄືນນີ້ ຂ້ອຍ ນອນ ບໍ່ ຄ່ອຍ ຫລັບ.

I didn't sleep very well last night.

10. mûu-kúun-nîi kɔ̀i nɔɔn lǎp dìi.

ມື້ຄືນນີ້ ຂ້ອຍ ນອນ ຫລັບ ດີ.

I slept very well last night.

11. A: kɔ̀i ngǎo-nɔɔn lǎai.

ຂ້ອຍ ເຫງົາ-ນອນ ຫລາຍ.

I'm really sleepy.

B: kɔi mɨai têɛ-têɛ.

ຂ້ອຍ ເມື່ອຍ ແຫ້ງໆ.

I'm really tired.

C: nùak-hŭu têɛ-têɛ.

ໜວກຫູ ແຫ້ງໆ.

It's really noisy.

D: dìi kak têɛ-têɛ .

ກໍ ຄັກ ແຫ້ງໆ .

It's really good.

12.   sĭang dàng lăai.

ສຽງ ດັງ ຫລາຍ.

The noise is very loud.

13.   láao fáng páa-săa láao bɔɔ tán.

ລາວ ຟັງ ພາສາ ລາວ ບໍ່ ທັນ.

He can't understand spoken Lao.

(Literally: He can't keep up with listening to the Lao language.)

14.   kɔi aan năng-sɨɨ láao bɔɔ ɔɔk.*

ຂ້ອຍ ອ່ານ ໜັງສື ລາວ ບໍ່ ອອກ.

I can't read Lao.

15.   kɔi gìn pĕt bɔɔ dâi.

ຂ້ອຍ ກິນ ເຜັດ ບໍ່ ໄດ້.

I can't eat hot food.

16.   kɔi bɔɔ dâi gìn pĕt.

ຂ້ອຍ ບໍ່ ໄດ້ ກິນ ເຜັດ.

I didn't eat hot food.

* ɔɔk is often used with the verbs, fáng, aan, kĭan.

  e.g. fáng bɔɔ ɔɔk. = fang bɔɔ dâi.

    I don't/can't understand. (I can't get what is being said.)

17.   kɔ̀i bpài mɯ́ang-láao bɔɔ dâi.
        ຂ້ອຍ ໄປ   ເມືອງລາວ   ບໍ່ ໄດ້.
        I can't go to Laos.

18.   kɔ̀i bɔɔ dâi bpài mɯ́ang láao.
        ຂ້ອຍ ບໍ່ ໄດ້   ໄປ ເມືອງ ລາວ.
        I didn't go to Laos.

19.   kɔ̀i kit-hɔ̂ɔt jâo lǎai.
        ຂ້ອຍ ຄຶດຮອດ ເຈົ້າ ຫລາຍ.
        I miss you very much.

20.   pûak-háo gàm-láng bɔng ta-lée.
        ພວກເຮົາ   ກຳລັງ   ເບິ່ງ ທະເລ.
        We are looking at the sea.

21.   kɔ̀i wâo páa-sǎa-láao bɔɔ kɔi tɯ̀ɯk.
        ຂ້ອຍ ເວົ້າ ພາສາລາວ   ບໍ່ ຄ່ອຍ ຖືກ.
        I don't speak Lao very correctly.

22.   láao aan páa-sǎa àng-gǐt dâi yaang bɔɔ pìt jǎk-dtòo lə̀əi.
        ລາວ ອ່ານ ພາສາ ອັງກິດ ໄດ້ ຢ່າງ ບໍ່ ຜິດ ຈັກໂຕ ເລີຍ.
        He reads English without making mistakes at all.
        (Literally: He reads English not incorrectly at all.)

23. A: kɔ̀i (kit) waa mán sɛ̂ɛp.
        ຂ້ອຍ (ຄຶດ) ວ່າ ມັນ ແຊບ.
        I think it's delicious.

     B: kɔ̀i kit waa àa-hǎan láao sɛ̂ɛp lǎai.
        ຂ້ອຍ ຄຶດ ວ່າ   ອາຫານ   ລາວ ແຊບ ຫລາຍ.
        I think Lao food is very delicious.

     C: kɔ̀i kit waa àa-hǎan láao sɛ̂ɛp ii-lǐi.
        ຂ້ອຍ ຄຶດ ວ່າ   ອາຫານ   ລາວ ແຊບ ອີ່ຫລີ.
        I think Lao food is really delicious.

     D: kɔ̀i kit waa mán pět.
        ຂ້ອຍ ຄຶດ ວ່າ   ມັນ ເຜັດ.
        I think it's spicy.

E: kòi kit waa àa-hǎan láao pět.

ຂ້ອຍ ຄິດ ວ່າ   ອາຫານ   ລາວ   ເຜັດ.

I think Lao food is spicy.

F: kòi kit waa àa-hǎan láao pět ii-lǐi.

ຂ້ອຍ ຄິດ ວ່າ   ອາຫານ   ລາວ   ເຜັດ ອີ່ຫລີ.

I think Lao food is really spicy.

24. A: jâo kit waa ja bpài mɯ́ang láao mɯa-dǎi.

ເຈົ້າ ຄິດ ວ່າ ຈະ ໄປ   ເມືອງ   ລາວ   ເມື່ອໃດ?

When do you think you will go to Laos?

B: kòi kit waa ja bpài dɯ̀an nàa.

ຂ້ອຍ ຄິດ ວ່າ ຈະ ໄປ   ເດືອນ ໜ້າ.

I think I will go next month.

25. A: láao sɯɯ ñǎng.

ລາວ   ຊື່ ຫຍັງ?

What's his name?

B: bɔɔ hûu. kòi kit bɔɔ ɔ̀ɔk.

ບໍ່ ຮູ້. ຂ້ອຍ ຄິດ ບໍ່ ອອກ.

I don't know. I can't think of it.

(Literally: I can't think it out.)

Test 7

Match the English words with the Lao words.

_____ 1. tired   a. pĭt ຜິດ

_____ 2. sleepy   b. ii-lǐi/kak/têɛ-têɛ
                                    ອີ່ຫລີ/ຄັກ/ແຫ້ແຫ້

_____ 3. to think about   c. som ສົ້ມ

_____ 4. to hear   d. kit-hɔ̂ɔt ຄິດຮອດ

_____ 5. sweet   e. dàng ດັງ

_____ 6. salty   f. sêɛp ແຊບ

_____ 7. incorrect   g. pĕt ເຜັດ

_____ 8. to remember   h. ngǎo-nɔ́ɔn ເຫງົານອນ

_____ 9. to finish   i. tùuk ຖືກ

_____ 10. delicious   j. wǎan ຫວານ

_____ 11. sour   k. lɛ̂ɛo ແລ້ວ

_____ 12. who   l. kit ຄິດ

_____ 13. loud   m. mʉai ເມື່ອຍ

_____ 14. really   n. kém ເຄັມ

_____ 15. correct   o. jʉu-dâi ຈັ່ໄດ້

                                   p. dâi-ñin ໄດ້ຍິນ

                                   q. pǎi ໃຜ

Translate the following into English.

1. bpûm-kĭan kɔ̌ɔng pǎi yuu táng dto.

   ປື້ມຮຽນ ຂອງ ໃຜ ຢູ່ ເທິງ ໂຕະ.

---

2. kɔ̀i lɔ́ɔi-nâam bɔɔ bpèn.

   ຂ້ອຍ ລອຍນ້ຳ ບໍ່ ເປັນ.

---

3. kɔ̀i bɔɔ dâi lɔ́ɔi-nâam.

   ຂ້ອຍ ບໍ່ ໄດ້ ລອຍນ້ຳ.

---

4. kɔ̀i kit hɔ̂ɔt mʉ́ang láao lǎai ii-lǐi.

   ຂ້ອຍ ຄິດ ຮອດ ເມືອງ ລາວ ຫລາຍ ອີ່ຫລີ.

---

5. kɔ̀i kit waa àa hǎan fa-lang bɔɔ kɔi sêɛp.

   ຂ້ອຍ ຄິດ ວ່າ ອາຫານ ຝຣັ່ງ ບໍ່ ຄ່ອຍ ແຊບ.

Tone Rules for Low Consonants (cont.)

In the absence of a tone mark, the tone rules for low consonants are as follows:

Low Consonant with <u>Live Syllable</u> = <u>High Tone</u>

Low Consonant with Long Vowel and <u>Dead Syllable</u> = <u>Falling Tone</u>

Low Consonant with Short Vowel and <u>Dead Syllable</u> = <u>Mid Tone</u>

Examples:

Low Consonant + Short Vowel = Mid Tone

	<u>Sound Produced</u>	<u>Meaning</u>
ພ + −ະ	= ພະ (pa)	monk
ລ + ເ−ະ	= ເລະ (le)	mushy

Exercise: Read the following words and practice writing them in Lao.

1.   ເຄາະ to knock

2.   ລະ to omit, per

3.   ເງາະ rambutan

4.   ແລະ and

5.   ແວະ to stop over

6.   ທຸລະ errand

Low Consonant + Any Vowel + <u>Sonorant Final</u>

= High Tone

	Sound Produced	Meaning
ລ + $\overset{\circ}{-}$ + ງ = ລີງ (líng)		monkey
ມ + $\overset{\smallfrown}{-}$ + ນ = ມັນ (mán)		it, potato
ຊ + −າ + ຍ = ຊາຍ (sáai)		sand

Low Consonant + <u>Long Vowel + Stop Final</u>

= Falling Tone

	Sound Produced	Meaning
ຄ + −າ + ບ = ຄາບ (kâap)		to hold something between the teeth
ລ + $\underset{ຸ}{-}$ + ກ = ລູກ (lûuk)		child
ມ + $\overset{\frown}{-}$ + ດ = ມີດ (mîit)		knife

Low Consonant + <u>Short Vowel + Stop Final</u>

= Mid Tone

	Sound Produced	Meaning
ຄ + $\overset{\smallfrown}{-}$ + ບ = ຄັບ (kap)		tight
ລ + $\underset{ຸ}{-}$ + ກ = ລຸກ (luk)		to rise, get up
ມ + $\overset{\circ}{-}$ + ດ = ມິດ (mit)		quiet

Exercise: Read the following words and practice writing them in Lao. Also identify the tones.

1. ລຸງ uncle

2. ມືດ dark

3. ເລກ math

4. ທານ alms

5. ທັບ to put on top

6. ນັດ appointment

7. ຮາດ to pour over

8. ຟາງ hay

9. ວັນ day

10. ລົບ to subtract

11. ຮັບ to receive

12. ຍັງ not yet, still

13. ໂລກ earth

14. ຊຸດ set

15. ນວດ to massage

16. ນາຍ boss

17. ພັງ to collapse

18. ທາກ snail

19. ຮັກ to love

20. ທຽມ fake

Tone Marks With Low Consonants

With low consonant syllables, there are three possible tones and two tone marks which may be used.

Tone Mark	Tone Name	Tone	Examples
—	sǐang sǎa-mán	mid	ຄາ (kaa)
—	sǐang tóo	falling	ຄ້າ (kâa)

The third possible tone, high tone, occurs with live syllables and no tone marks. (Review "Tone Rules for Low Consonants" on page 158.)

Exercise: Read the following words and practice writing them in Lao. Also identify the tones.

1. ມ່ວງ purple

2. ມັນ that

3. ຊີ້ນ meat

4. ຊັ້ນ grade, floor

5. ຟ້າ sky

6. ຄ້າງ to remain

7. ລົ້ນ to overflow

8. ມ້າ horse

9. ນີ້ this

10. ພໍ່ term of endearment for an older person

Read The Following Aloud

1. ກາ   ກ່າ   ກ້າ

2. ຢຸ   ຢຸ່   ຢຸ້

3. ຢູ   ຢູ່   ຢູ້

4. ແຫ   ແຫ່   ແຫ້

5. ໄພ   ໄພ່   ໄພ້

6. ເມົາ   ເມົ່າ   ເມົ້າ

7. ຫຳ   ຫ່ຳ   ຫ້ຳ

8. ໄມ   ໄມ່   ໄມ້

9. ແຍ   ແຍ່   ແຍ້

10. ຣື   ຣື່   ຣື້

11. ເລັຍ   ເລ່ຍ   ເລ້ຍ

12. ໂວ   ໂວ່   ໂວ້

Writing Exercise 7

Transcribe the following into Lao script.

1. muang _____

2. nok _____

3. kam _____

4. ñúung _____

5. fíim _____

6. nîu _____

7. mîit _____

8. sɔ́ɔng _____

9. fáng _____

10. wέεo _____

11. sáam _____

12. hîap _____

13. púum _____

14. hâan _____

15. hâap _____

16. wâang _____

17. ñ̂ɯang _____

18. sεng _____

19. kok _____

20. p̂ɯa _____

Lesson 8

body parts; everyday life; silent ห (hɔ̌ɔ)

bŏt-tíi bpèet ບົດທີ ແປດ Lesson 8

kám-săp ຄຳສັບ Vocabulary

dtàa	ຕາ	eye
hŭu	ຫູ	ear
dàng	ດັງ	nose
bpàak	ປາກ	mouth
kèo	ແຂ້ວ	tooth
lín	ລີ້ນ	tongue
nùat	ໜວດ	mustache
káo	ເຄົາ	beard
gêɛm-bɔng	ແກ້ມບ່ອງ	dimple
kíu	ຄິ້ວ	eyebrow
pŏm	ຜົມ	hair (on the head only)
kŏn	ຂົນ	hair
kŏn-dtàa	ຂົນຕາ	eyelash
hŭa	ຫົວ	head
nàa	ໜ້າ	face
nàa-pàak	ໜ້າຜາກ	forehead
lăng	ຫຼັງ	back
kɔ́ɔ	ຄໍ	neck
tɔ̂ɔng	ທ້ອງ	stomach
săai bùu	ສາຍບື	navel
hŭa-jài	ຫົວໃຈ	heart
nóm	ນົມ	breast
ŏk	ເອິກ	chest
múu	ມື	hand
nîu/nîu-múu	ນິ້ວ/ ນິ້ວມື	finger
lep-múu	ເລັບມື	nail

kɛ̌ɛn ແຂນ	arm
kǎa ຂາ	leg
hǔa-kao ຫົວເຂົ່າ	knee
dtìin ຕີນ	foot
nîu-dtìin ນິ້ວຕີນ	toe
fǎi/bpàan ໄຝ/ປານ	mole
sǐu ສິວ	pimple
nâam-dtàa ນ້ຳຕາ	tear
sa-mɔ̌ɔng ສະໝອງ	brain
dtǎp ຕັບ	liver
màak-kai-lǎng ໝາກໄຂ່ຫຼັງ	kidney
sài ໃສ້	intestine
tɔ̂ɔng-nɔ̂ɔi ທ້ອງນ້ອຍ	fat stomach, paunch
ga-dùuk ກະດູກ	bone
haang-gàai ຮ່າງກາຍ	body
sɯ̂ɯ-kɯang ຊື້ເຄື່ອງ	to shop, to buy things
bpài sɯ̂ɯ-kɯang ໄປຊື້ເຄື່ອງ	to go shopping
sai/nung ໃສ່/ນຸ່ງ	to wear, put on
tɔ̌ɔt/bpǒt ຖອດ/ປົດ	to take off
dtɛng-dtùa ແຕ່ງຕົວ	to get dressed
bpùat ປວດ	to ache
jěp ເຈັບ	to hurt
bpèn-wǎt ເປັນຫວັດ	to catch a cold
dtǎt ຕັດ	to cut
tɛ̌ɛ ແຖ	to shave
lâang ລ້າງ	to wash
sǎ-pǒm ສະຜົມ	to wash hair
àap-nâm/àap-nâam ອາບນ້ຳ	to take a bath or a shower
sak-kɯang-nung ຊັກເຄື່ອງນຸ່ງ	to do the laundry
tǔu kɛ̀o ຖູແຂ້ວ	to brush one's teeth

bpɛ̀ɛng-tǔu-kɛ̀o	ແປງຖູແຂ້ວ	toothbrush
yàa-tǔu-kɛ̀o	ຢາຖູແຂ້ວ	toothpaste
sa-bùu	ສະບູ	soap
fɛɛp	ແຟບ	detergent
mùak	ໝວກ	hat
sùa	ເສື້ອ	shirt, blouse
sùa-yʉ̂ʉt	ເສື້ອຍືດ	T-shirt
sùa-ñai	ເສື້ອໃຫຍ່	business suit
sùa-kɛ̌ɛn-ñáao	ເສື້ອແຂນຍາວ	long-sleeved shirt
sùa-kɛ̌ɛn-sàn	ເສື້ອແຂນສັ້ນ	short-sleeved shirt
gàa-la-wat	ກາລະວັດ	necktie
sǎai-ɛ̀ɛo	ສາຍແອວ	belt
kěm-mǔt	ເຂັມໝຸດ	pin, brooch
gɔ̀ɔp	ເກີບ	shoe
tǒng-dtìin	ຖົງຕີນ	sock
tǒng-mʉ́ʉ	ຖົງມື	glove
sòng-sɔ̀ɔn-kǎa-ñáao	ໂສ້ງຂ້ອນຂາຍາວ	panty hose
ga-bpoong	ກະໂປ່ງ	skirt
sòng	ໂສ້ງ	trousers
dtûm-hǔu	ຕຸ້ມຫູ	earring
wɛ̌ɛn	ແຫວນ	ring
gông-kɛ̌ɛn/sǎai-kɛ̌ɛn	ກ້ອງແຂນ/ສາຍແຂນ	bracelet
sɔ̀i-kɔ̌ɔ/sǎai-kɔ̌ɔ	ສາຍສ້ອຍ/ສາຍຄໍ	necklace
bòo	ໂບ	ribbon
kɔ̌ɔng/kuang	ຂອງ/ເຄື່ອງ	thing
dtɛ̀ɛ-la/dtɔɔ	ແຕ່ລະ/ຕໍ່	per
kâap/kâng	ຄາບ/ຄັ້ງ	time
bpèn-ñǎng	ເປັນຫຍັງ?	"What's the matter?"
kóng/kóng-jǎ/kʉ̀ʉ-si	ຄົງ/ຄົງຈະ/ຄືຊິ	may, maybe

Conversation

Ron: ma-níi sà-baai-dii bɔɔ.

ຣອນ: ມະນີ,   ສະບາຍດີ   ບໍ່?

      Manee, how are you doing?

Manee: kɔ̀i bɔɔ kɔi sa-bàai bpàan-dǎi.*

ມະນີ:   ຂ້ອຍ ບໍ່ ຄ່ອຍ ສະບາຍ ປານໃດ.

      I'm not so well.   (*Not so much.)

Ron: bpèn-ñǎng.

ຣອນ: ເປັນຫຍັງ?

      What's the matter?

Manee: mûu-nîi kɔ̀i jĕp hǔa lǎai. kit waa kúu si bpèn wǎt.

ມະນີ:   ມື້ນີ້ ຂ້ອຍ ເຈັບ ຫົວ ຫລາຍ. ຄິດ ວ່າ ຄື ຊິ ເປັນ ຫວັດ.

      Today I have a bad headache. I think I may have a cold.

Ron: jâo bpài hóong-mɔ̌ɔ lɛ̂ɛo bɔɔ.

ຣອນ: ເຈົ້າ ໄປ   ໂຮງໝໍ ແລ້ວ ບໍ່?

      Have you gone to see a doctor (to the hospital)?

Manee: ñáng-tʉa. kit-waa mûu-ʉʉn jʉng** ja bpài.

ມະນີ:   ຍັງເທື່ອ.   ຄິດວ່າ ມື້ອື່ນ   ຈຶ່ງ   ຈະ ໄປ.

      Not yet. I will go tomorrow.

       (** jʉng is used for emphasis.)

      táan lɔ́ɔn sa-bàai dìi bɔɔ.

      ທ່ານ ຣອນ   ສະບາຍ ດີ ບໍ່?

      How are you doing, Ron?

Ron: sa-bàai dìi. dtɛɛ-waa àa-tit lɛ̂ɛo jĕp kɛ̀o nɔ̀i-nʉng.

ຣອນ: ສະບາຍ ດີ.   ແຕ່ວ່າ   ອາທິດ ແລ້ວ ເຈັບ ແຂ້ວ ໜ້ອຍນຶ່ງ.

      I'm fine. But last week I had a little bit of a toothache.

Manee: mûu-nîi jâo ja het ñǎng.

ມະນີ:   ມື້ນີ້ ເຈົ້າ ຈະ ເຮັດ ຫຍັງ?

What will you do today?

Ron: kɔ̀i ja bpài sɨ̂u-kɨang yuu dta-làat sâo.***

ຣອນ: ຂ້ອຍ ຈະ ໄປ ຊື້ເຄື່ອງ ຢູ່ ຕະຫລາດເຊົ້າ.

I will go shopping at Morning Market .

(*** Main shopping area of Vientiene.)

Manee: jâo ja sɨ̂u ñǎng.

ມະນີ:   ເຈົ້າ ຈະ ຊື້ ຫຍັງ?

What will you buy?

Ron: kɔ̀i yàak sɨ̂u sɨ̀a gǎp gɔ̀əp.

ຣອນ: ຂ້ອຍ ຢາກ ຊື້ ເສື້ອ ກັບ ເກີບ.

I want to buy shirts and shoes.

bpà-ñòok   ปะໄທຍກ   **Sentences**

1. A: pûak-háo gamlang nung sửa yuu.

   ພວກ ເຮົາ ກຳລັງ ນຸ່ງ ເສື້ອ ຢູ່.

   We are wearing (putting on) our shirts.

   B: láao nung sửa-ñai sǐi fâa-gɛɛ lɛ mat gàa-la-wat sǐi dɛ̀ɛng.

   ລາວ ນຸ່ງ ເສື້ອໃຫຍ່ ສີ ຟ້າແກ່ ແລະ ມັດ ກາລະວັດ ສີ ແດງ.

   He is wearing a blue business jacket and a red necktie.

2. A: láao nung sửa sǐi ñǎng.

   ລາວ ນຸ່ງ ເສື້ອ ສີ ຫຍັງ?

   What color shirt is he wearing?

   B: láao nung sửa sǐi kǎao.

   ລາວ ນຸ່ງ ເສື້ອ ສີ ຂາວ.

   He is wearing a white shirt.

3. mûu-uun kɔ̀i ja bpài dtǎt pǒm.

   ມື້ອື່ນ ຂ້ອຍ ຈະ ໄປ ຕັດ ຜົມ.

   Tomorrow I will go get a haircut.

4. kɔ̀i tɛ́ɛ nùat tuk sâo.

   ຂ້ອຍ ແຖ ຫນວດ ທຸກ ເຊົ້າ.

   I shave my mustache every morning.

5. kón láao mak àap-nâm.

   ຄົນ ລາວ ມັກ ອາບນ້ຳ.

   Lao people like to take baths.

6. A: jâo gìn kào mûu la jǎk kâap.

   ເຈົ້າ ກິນ ເຂົ້າ ມື້ ລະ ຈັກ ຄາບ?

   How many times a day do you eat a meal?

   B: kɔ̀i gìn kào mûu la sǎam kâap.

   ຂ້ອຍ ກິນ ເຂົ້າ ມື້ ລະ ສາມ ຄາບ.

   I eat three times a day.

7. A: jâo sak kɯang-nung àa-tit la jǎk tɯa.

   ເຈົ້າ ຊັກ ເຄື່ອງນຸ່ງ ອາທິດ ລະ ຈັກ ເທື່ອ?

   How many times a week do you do the laundry?

   B: kɔ̀i sak kɯang-nung àa-tit la sɔ̌ɔng tɯa.

   ຂ້ອຍ ຊັກ ເຄື່ອງນຸ່ງ ອາທິດ ລະ ສອງ ເທື່ອ.

   I do the laundry twice a week.

8. mɯ̂ɯ-nîi kɔ̀i jěp kɛ̀o lǎai tɛ̂ɛ-tɛ̂ɛ.

    ມື້ນີ້ ຂ້ອຍ ເຈັບ ແຂ້ວ ຫລາຍ ແທ້ໆ.

    Today I really have a bad toothache.

9. kɔ̀i ja bpài lâang mɯ́ɯ yuu hɔ̀ng-nâm.

    ຂ້ອຍ ຈະ ໄປ ລ້າງ ມື ຢູ່ ຫ້ອງນ້ຳ.

    I will go wash my hands in the bathroom.

10. kɔ̀i yàak mîi nùat.

    ຂ້ອຍ ຢາກ ມີ ໜວດ.

    I want to have a mustache.

11. jěp hǔa-kao.

    ເຈັບ ຫົວເຂົ່າ.

    My knees hurt.

12. pûak-háo mîi nîu-mɯ́ɯ hàa nîu.

    ພວກເຮົາ ມີ ນິ້ວມື ຫ້າ ນິ້ວ.

    We have five fingers.

13. kɔ̀i ja bpài sɯ̀ɯ sa-bùu gǎp yàa-sǐi-kɛ̀o.

    ຂ້ອຍ ຈະ ໄປ ຊື້ ສະບູ ກັບ ຢາສີແຂ້ວ.

    I will go to buy soap and toothpaste.

14. láao mak nung sɯ̀a-kɛ̌ɛn-ñáao.

    ລາວ ມັກ ນຸ່ງ ເສື້ອແຂນຍາວ.

    He likes to wear long sleeved shirts.

15. tɔ̀ɔng láao ñai nɔ̀i-nɯng.

    ທ້ອງ ລາວ ໃຫຍ່ ໜ້ອຍນຶ່ງ.

    He has a little paunch.

Test 8

Match the English words with the Lao words.

_____ 1.	hand	a. gɔ̀ɔp ເກັບ
_____ 2.	to wash	b. hǔu ຫູ
_____ 3.	face	c. kǎa ຂາ
_____ 4.	to take a bath	d. múu ມື
_____ 5.	head	e. hǔa ຫົວ
_____ 6.	to cut	f. jěp ເຈັບ
_____ 7.	leg	g. ga-bpoong ກະໂປ່ງ
_____ 8.	shoe	h. àap-nâam ອາບນ້ຳ
_____ 9.	skirt	i. nàa ໜ້າ
_____ 10.	hair	j. sak-kʉang-nung ຊັກເຄື່ອງນຸ່ງ
_____ 11.	hat	k. mùak ໝວກ
_____ 12.	ear	l. sa-bùu ສະບູ
_____ 13.	soap	m. lâang ລ້າງ
_____ 14.	to do the laundry	n. pǒm ຜົມ
_____ 15.	to have pain	o. tǒng-dtìin ກົງຕີນ
		p. dtǎt ຕັດ
		q. sòng ໂສ້ງ

Translate the following into English.

1. A: jâo tŭu kèo wán la jăk tɯa.

    ເຈົ້າ ຖຸ ແຂ້ວ ວັນ ລະ ຈັກ ເທື່ອ.

    _____

    B: wán la sɔ̌ɔng tɯa.

    ວັນ ລະ ສອງ ເທື່ອ.

    _____

2. láao jěp hŭa lăai. láao máa het wîak bɔɔ dâi.

    ລາວ ເຈັບ ຫົວ ຫລາຍ. ລາວ ມາ ເຮັດ ວຽກ ບໍ່ ໄດ້.

    _____

3. kɔ̀i sǎ-pŏm tuk mɯ̂ɯ.

    ຂ້ອຍ ສະຜົມ ທຸກ ມື້.

    _____

4. sŏm-sŭk míi gêɛm-bong.

    ສົມສຸກ ມີ ແກ້ມບ່ອງ.

    _____

5. jâo bɔɔ míi sa-mɔ̌ɔng.

    ເຈົ້າ ບໍ່ ມີ ສະໝອງ.

    _____

Silent ຫ

A silent ຫ is called "hɔ̌ɔ-nám." It may appear before the following six low consonants. In this case, the low consonant takes on all the tone characteristics of the high consonant ຫ. When a tone mark appears, it is placed over the low consonant, not over the silent ຫ.

1. ງ (ຫງ)

2. ຍ (ຫຍ)

3. ນ (ຫນ or ຫນ)

4. ມ (ຫມ or ຫມ)

5. ລ (ຫຼ or ຫລ)

6. ວ (ຫວ)

		Sound Produced	Meaning
ຫ + ງອກ	=	ຫງອກ (ngɔ̀ɔk)	gray hair
ຫ + ຍ້າ	=	ຫຍ້າ (yàa)	grass
ຫ + ນີ້	=	ຫນີ້ (nìi)	debt
ຫ + ມາ	=	ຫມາ (mǎa)	dog
ຫ + ລາຍ	=	ຫຼາຍ, ຫລາຍ (lǎai)	many
ຫ + ວານ	=	ຫວ່ານ (waan)	to sow

In syllables with the silent high consonant ຫ, all high consonant tone rules apply. (See pages 102 and 121.)

Tone Mark	Tone Name	Tone	Examples
None	sĭang jàt-dtà-waa	rising	ໝາ (mǎa)
່	sĭang sǎa-mán	mid	ໝ່າ (maa)
້	sĭang èek	low	ໝ້າ (màa)

Exercise: Read the following words and practice writing them in Lao. Also identify the tones.

1. ຫຼື or

2. ໂหລ dozen

3. ຫນູ rat

4. ໝູ pig

5. ໝ້າ face

6. ຫວານ sweet

7. ໝອນ pillow

8. ຫลับ asleep

9. ຫยัງ what

10. ຫງາย face up

Read The Following Aloud

1 . ຫມ່າ   ຫມ້າ   ຫມາ

2 . ຫມ່ີ   ຫມ້ີ   ຫມິ

3 . ເຫງ່   ເຫງ້   ເຫງ

4 . ໄຫລ່   ໄຫລ້   ໄຫລ

5 . ເຫວ່າ   ເຫວ້າ   ເຫວາ

6 . ຫຍ່າ   ຫຍ້າ   ຫຍາ

Writing Exercise 8

Transcribe the following into Lao script using ທ ນ້ຳ /hɔ̌ɔ-nám/.

1. mii _____   6. lǎa _____

2. nǎi _____   7. wuu _____

3. ñai _____   8. loong _____

4. nìi _____   9. wan _____

5. man _____   10. wǎa _____

Lesson 9

family and kinship terms; occupations; animals;
punctuation marks; practice reading short sentences

bŏt-tíi gâo   ບົດທີ ເກົ້າ   Lesson 9

kám-săp   ຄຳສັບ   Vocabulary

sŭan	ສວນ	garden
sŭan-săt	ສວນສັດ	zoo
àa-ñu	ອາຍຸ	age
bɔ̀ɔ-li-săt	ບໍລິສັດ	company
bpèn ñăng	ເປັນຫຍັງ	why
pɔ-waa/tîi-wɔ̀ɔn-wâa	ເພາະວ່າ/ຍ້ອນວ່າ	because
tàa/tàa-hàak	ຖ້າ/ຖ້າຫາກ	if
dteng-ngáan/dteng-dɔ̀ɔng		to get married, to marry
ແຕ່ງງານ/ແຕ່ງດອງ		
sòot	ໂສດ	single
hak	ຮັກ	to love
táng-sɔ̌ɔng	ທັງສອງ	both

kɔ̂p-kúa   ຄອບຄົວ   Family

puu-sáai	ຜູ້ຊາຍ	man, male
puu-ñíng	ຜູ້ຍິງ	woman, female
puu-ñai	ຜູ້ໃຫຍ່	adult
děk-nɔ̂ɔi/lûuk	ເດັກນ້ອຍ/ລູກ	child
lûuk-sáai	ລູກຊາຍ	son
lûuk-sǎao	ລູກສາວ	daughter
sǎa-míi	ສາມີ	husband
pán-la-ñáa	ພັນລະຍາ	wife
pǔa	ຜົວ	husband
mía	ເມຍ/ເມັຍ	wife

pɔɔ ພໍ່	father
mɛɛ ແມ່	mother
âai-ûai ອ້າຍເອື້ອຍ	older sibling
nɔ̂ɔng ນ້ອງ	younger sibling
âai ອ້າຍ	older brother
ûai ເອື້ອຍ	older sister
nɔ̂ɔng-sáai ນ້ອງຊາຍ	younger brother
nɔ̂ɔng-sǎao ນ້ອງສາວ	younger sister
bpuu ປູ່	father's father
ñaa ຍ່າ	father's mother
pɔɔ-tào ພໍ່ເຖົ້າ	mother's father
mɛɛ-tào ແມ່ເຖົ້າ	mother's mother
lúng ລຸງ	father or mother's older brother
bpâa ປ້າ	father or mother's older sister
nâa-baao/nâa-sǎao ນ້າບ່າວ/ນ້າສາວ	mother's younger brother or sister
àao ອາວ	father's younger brother
àa ອາ	father's younger sister

àa-sìip ອາຊີບ **Occupations**

kúu/àa-jàan ຄູ/ອາຈານ	teacher, professor
taan-mɔ̌ɔ ທ່ານໝໍ	doctor
(taan)-mɔ̌ɔ-bpùa-kɛo (ທ່ານ) ໝໍປົວແຂ້ວ	dentist
nak-tu-la-gìt ນັກທຸລະກິດ	businessman
nak-sǔk-sǎa ນັກສຶກສາ	college student

nak-hían   ນັກຮຽນ   student

nak-kían   ນັກຂຽນ   writer

nak-bìn   ນັກບິນ   pilot

nak-hɔ̂ɔng   ນັກຮ້ອງ   singer

nak-sùup   ນັກສືບ   spy

nak-ɔ̀ɔk-bèɛp   ນັກອອກແບບ   designer

pa-nak-ngáan-lat   ພະນັກງານລັດ   government official

wit-sa-wa-gɔ̀ɔn   ວິສະວະກອນ   engineer

dtàm-lùat   ຕຳຫລວດ   policeman

ta-hǎan   ທະຫານ   soldier

pa-ñáa-bàan   ພະຍາບານ   nurse

kón-kǎp-lot   ຄົນຂັບລົດ   driver

saang-(jǎk)   ຊ່າງ (ຈັກ)   mechanic

saang-dtǎt-pǒm   ຊ່າງຕັດຜົມ   barber

sáao-náa   ຊາວນາ   farmer

pa/kúu-bàa   ພະ/ຄູບາ   monk

lée-kǎa   ເລຂາ   secretary

mɛɛ-bâan/mɛɛ-húan   housewife
ແມ່ບ້ານ/ ແມ່ເຮືອນ

pɔɔ-kâa/mɛɛ-kâa   ພໍ່ຄ້າ/ ແມ່ຄ້າ   merchant

dàa-láa   ດາລາ   movie star

jâo-kɔ̌ɔng   ເຈົ້າຂອງ   owner

jâo-kɔ̌ɔng-hâan   ເຈົ້າຂອງຮ້ານ   shop owner

jâo-kɔ̌ɔng tu-la-gǐt   ເຈົ້າຂອງທຸລະກິດ   business owner

het-wîak kɔ̌ɔng dtòn-èeng   self-employed
ເຮັດວຽກຂອງຕົນເອງ

het-wîak nám bɔ̀ɔ-li-sǎt   ເຮັດວຽກນຳບໍລິສັດ company employee

nak-bpûn/jòon-bpûn   ນັກປຸ້ນ/ໂຈມປຸ້ນ   robber

ka-móoi/jòon/kón-kìi-lak   thief
ຂະໂມຍ/ໂຈມ/ຄົນຂີ້ລັກ

săt ສັດ **Animals**

săt-ĺiang	ສັດລ້ຽງ	pet
dtòo-pùu/dtòo-tɔ̀ək	ໂຕຜູ້/ໂຕເຖິກ	male (animal)
dtòo-mɛɛ	ໂຕແມ່	female (animal)
mǎa	ໝາ	dog
mέɛo	ແມວ	cat
mǔu	ໝູ	pig
bpĕt	ເປັດ	duck
gai/gai-mɛɛ	ໄກ່/ໄກ່ແມ່	chicken, hen
sâang	ຊ້າງ	elephant
mâa	ມ້າ	horse
ngúa	ງົວ	cow, ox
kwáai	ຄວາຍ	buffalo
bpùu	ປູ	crab
bpàa	ປາ	fish
hɔ̌i	ຫອຍ	shell, oyster, etc.
gûng	ກຸ້ງ	shrimp
nok	ນົກ	bird
ĺing	ລິງ	monkey
nǔu	ໝູ	rat, mouse
ngúu	ງູ	snake
sǔa	ເສືອ	tiger
sǐng-dtòo	ສິງໂຕ	lion
kὲɛ	ແຂ້	crocodile
dtao	ເຕົ່າ	turtle
dtoo-jing-jôo	ໂຕຈິງໂຈ້	kangaroo
bὲɛ	ແບ້	goat
gĕ	ແກະ	sheep
mǐi	ໝີ	bear
ùut	ອູດ	camel

jia ເຈຍ	bat
màa-láai ມ້າລາຍ	zebra
măa-bpaa/măa-nái ໝາປ່າ/ໝາໄມ	wolf
măa-jɔɔk ໝາຈອກ	fox
mɛ́ɛng-ga-bùa ແມງກະເບື້ອ	butterfly
mot ມົດ	ant
ñúng ຍຸງ	mosquito
mɛ́ɛng-wán ແມງວັນ	fly

Conversation

Ann: kúun, jâo dtɛng-ngáan lɛ̂ɛo bɔɔ.

ແອນ: ຄູນ, ເຈົ້າ ແຕ່ງງານ ແລ້ວ ບໍ່?

Kuun, are you married?

Kuun: dtɛng lɛ̂ɛo. mía kɔ̀i sʉʉ wi-lái.

ຄູນ: ແຕ່ງ ແລ້ວ. ເມຍ ຂ້ອຍ ຊື່ ວິໄລ.

Yes. My wife's name is Wilai.

Ann: jâo míi lùuk lɛ̂ɛo bɔɔ.

ແອນ: ເຈົ້າ ມີ ລູກ ແລ້ວ ບໍ່?

Do you have children?

Kuun: míi lɛ̂ɛo, sɔ̌ɔng kón. ñíng nʉng, sáai nʉng.

ຄູນ: ມີ ແລ້ວ. ສອງ ຄົນ, ຍິງ ນຶ່ງ, ຊາຍ ນຶ່ງ.

I have two, one girl and one boy.

Ann: jâo het wìak ñăng.

ແອນ: ເຈົ້າ ເຣັດ ວຽກ ຫຍັງ?

What kind of work do you do?

Kuun: kɔ̀i het wìak yuu ta-náa-káan.

ຄູນ: ຂ້ອຍ ເຣັດ ວຽກ ຢູ່ ທະນາຄານ.

I work at a bank.

Ann: ta-náa-káan dǎi.

ແອນ: ທະນາຄານ ໃດ?

What bank?

Kuun: ta-náa-káan láao-mai.

ຄູນ: ທະນາຄານ   ລາວໃໝ່.

New Lao Bank.

ɛ̂ɛn, jâo het wîak ñǎng.

ແອນ, ເຈົ້າ ເຮັດ ວຽກ ຫຍັງ?

What kind of work do you do, Ann?

Ann: kɔ̀i het tu-la-gǐt kɔ̌ɔng kɔ̀i eeng yuu àa-mée-li-gàa.

ແອນ: ຂ້ອຍ ເຮັດ ທຸລະກິດ ຂອງ ຂ້ອຍ ເອງ ຢູ່ ອາເມລິກາ.

I work for myself in America.

Kuun: jâo dtɛng-ngáan lɛ̂ɛo bɔɔ.

ຄູນ: ເຈົ້າ   ແຕ່ງງານ   ແລ້ວ ບໍ່?

Are you married?

Ann: ñǎng.   kɔ̀i ñǎng bɔɔ tán mǐi féen tʉa.

ແອນ: ຍັງ.   ຂ້ອຍ ຍັງ ບໍ່ ທັນ ມີ ແຟນ ເທື່ອ.

Not yet. I don't have a boyfriend yet.

bpà-ñòok ປະໂຫຍກ **Sentences**

1. A: kɔ̂ɔp-kúa jâo mîi jǎk kón.

   ຄອບ ຄົວ ເຈົ້າ ມີ ຈັກ ຄົນ?

   How many people are there in your family?

   B: mîi jět kón. mîi pɔɔ, mɛɛ, âai, ûai,

   ມີ ເຈັດ ຄົນ. ມີ ພໍ່, ແມ່, ອ້າຍ, ເອື້ອຍ,

   nɔ̂ɔng-sáai sɔ̌ɔng kón gǎp kɔ̀i.

   ນ້ອງຊາຍ ສອງ ຄົນ ກັບ ຂ້ອຍ.

   There are seven—my father, mother, older brother,

   older sister, two younger brothers and me.

2. A: pùu-nân mɛɛn pǎi.

   ຜູ້ນັ້ນ ແມ່ນ ໃຜ?

   Who is that?

   B: pùu-nân mɛɛn nɔ̂ɔng-sǎao kɔ̀i.

   ຜູ້ນັ້ນ ແມ່ນ ນ້ອງສາວ ຂ້ອຍ.

   That is my younger sister.

3. A: âai jâo het wîak ñǎng.

   ອ້າຍ ເຈົ້າ ເຮັດ ວຽກ ຫຍັງ?

   What kind of work does your older brother do?

   B: láao bpèn witsa-wa-gɔ̀ɔn.

   ລາວ ເປັນ ວິສະອະກອນ.

   He is an engineer.

   A: jâo het wîak ñǎng.

   ເຈົ້າ ເຮັດ ວຽກ ຫຍັງ?

   What kind of work do you do?

B: kɔ̀i het wîak yuu bɔ̀ɔ-li-sǎt.

ຂ້ອຍ ເຮັດ ວຽກ ຢູ່ ບໍລິສັດ.

I work for a company.

4. A: láao het wîak ñǎng.

ລາວ ເຮັດ ວຽກ ຫຍັງ?

What is his occupation?

B: láao bpèn kúu sɔ̌ɔn páa-sǎa láao.

ລາວ ເປັນ ຄູ ສອນ ພາສາ ລາວ.

He is a Lao teacher.

5. A: jâo dtɛng-ngáan lɛ̂ɛo bɔɔ.

ເຈົ້າ ແຕ່ງງານ ແລ້ວ ບໍ?

Are you married yet?

B: dtɛ̀ng lɛ̂ɛo.

ແຕ່ງ ແລ້ວ.

Yes, I am.

C: ñáng, ñáng bɔɔ tán dtɛng. kɔ̀i ñáng bpen sòot yuu.

ຍັງ, ຍັງ ບໍ່ ທັນ ແຕ່ງ. ຂ້ອຍ ຍັງ ເປັນ ໂສດ ຢູ່.

No, I'm not. I'm still single.

6. A: jâo míi lûuk jǎk kón.

ເຈົ້າ ມີ ລູກ ຈັກ ຄົນ?

How many children do you have?

B: sɔ̌ɔng kón.   bpèn pùu-sáai táng sɔ̌ɔng kón.

ສອງ ຄົນ. ເປັນ ຜູ້ຊາຍ ທັງ ສອງ ຄົນ.

Two. Both of them are boys.

7. A: jâo àa-ñu tao-dǎi./jâo àa-ñu jǎk bpìi.

ເຈົ້າ ອາຍຸ ເທົ່າໃດ?/ເຈົ້າ ອາຍຸ ຈັກ ປີ?

How old are you?

B: săam-sĭp bpìi.

ສາມສິບ ປີ.

Thirty years old.

A: ûai jâo àa-ñu tao-dǎi.

ເອື້ອຍ ເຈົ້າ ອາຍຸ ເທົ່າໃດ?

How old is your older sister?

B: săam-sĭp-sii.

ສາມສິບສີ່.

Thirty-four.

8. A: hŭan jâo míi săt-ĺiang bɔɔ.

ເຮືອນ ເຈົ້າ ມີ ສັດລ້ຽງ ບໍ?

Do you have pets at home?

B: míi. míi măa găp mέεo.

ມີ. ມີ ໝາ ກັບ ແມວ.

Yes, I have a dog and a cat.

9. A: păi bpèn kúu sɔ̌ɔn páa-săa láao.

ໃຜ ເປັນ ຄູ ສອນ ພາສາ ລາວ?

Who is the Lao teacher?

B: taan sɔ̌ɔn bpèn kúu sɔ̌ɔn páa-săa láao.

ທ່ານ ສອນ ເປັນ ຄູ ສອນ ພາສາ ລາວ.

Mr. Sorn is the Lao teacher.

10. A: jâo het wĭak găp bɔɔ-li-săt ñăng.

ເຈົ້າ ເຮັດ ວຽກ ກັບ ບໍລິສັດ ຫຍັງ?

What company do you work with?

B: het găp bɔɔ-li-săt ñii-bpun.

ເຮັດ ກັບ ບໍລິສັດ ຍີ່ປຸ່ນ.

With a Japanese company.

11. A: bpèn ñăng jâo juŋ hían páa-săa láao.

ເປັນ ຫຍັງ ເຈົ້າ ຈຶ່ງ ຮຽນ ພາສາ ລາວ?

Why do you study Lao?

B: pɔ-waa kɔ̀i mak kón láao lăai.

ເພາະວ່າ ຂ້ອຍ ມັກ ຄົນ ລາວ ຫລາຍ.

Because I like Lao people very much.

12. A: àa-tit lɛ̂ɛo bpèn ñăng jâo juŋ bɔɔ máa wat.

ອາທິດ ແລ້ວ ເປັນ ຫຍັງ ເຈົ້າ ຈຶ່ງ ບໍ່ ມາ ວັດ?

Why didn't you come to the temple last week?

B: prɔ-waa kɔ̀i bɔɔ kɔi sa-bàai.

ເພາະວ່າ ຂ້ອຍ ບໍ່ ຄ່ອຍ ສະບາຍ.

Because I wasn't feeling well.

13. A: tàa jâo míi ngén lăai lăai, jâo yàak jă het ñăng.

ຖ້າ ເຈົ້າ ມີ ເງິນ ຫລາຍໆ, ເຈົ້າ ຢາກ ຈະ ເຮັດ ຫຍັງ?

If you had a lot of money, what would you do?

B: kɔ̀i jă sɯ̂ɯ húan yuu múang láao.

ຂ້ອຍ ຈະ ຊື້ ເຮືອນ ຢູ່ ເມືອງ ລາວ.

I would buy a house in Laos.

14. A: tàa fŏn dtŏk, jâo jă het jang dăi.

ຖ້າ ຝົນ ຕົກ ເຈົ້າ ຈະ ເຮັດ ຈັ່ງ ໃດ?

If it rains, what (how) will you do?

B: kɔ̀i gɔɔ jă bɔɔ bpài het wîak.

ຂ້ອຍ ກໍ່ ຈະ ບໍ່ ໄປ ເຮັດ ວຽກ.

I won't go to work.

15.   mɯ̂ɯ-nîi kɔ̀i jép kɛ̀o lăai.   kɔ̀i yàak bpài-hăa mɔ̆ɔ-bpua-kɛ̀o.

ມື້ນີ້ ຂ້ອຍ ເຈັບ ແຂ້ວ ຫລາຍ. ຂ້ອຍ ຢາກ ໄປຫາ ໝໍປົວແຂ້ວ.

Today I have a bad toothache. I want to see a dentist.

16.   kɔ̀i kit waa láao bpèn nak tu-la-gǐt jàak ñii-bpun.

ຂ້ອຍ ຄິດ ວ່າ ລາວ ເປັນ ນັກ ທຸລະກິດ ຈາກ ຍີ່ປຸ່ນ.

I think he is a businessman from Japan.

17.   yuu nìi mɨ́i jɔ̀on lǎai tɛ̂ɛ-tɛ̂ɛ.

ຢູ່ ນີ້ ມີ ໂຈນ ຫລາຍ ແທ້ໆ.

This place really has a lot of thieves.

18. A: kɔ̀i mɨ́i lúng yuu tii àng-gǐt.

ຂ້ອຍ ມີ ລຸງ ຢູ່ ທີ່ ອັງກິດ.

I have an uncle in England.

B: láao mɨ́i kɔ̀ɔp-kúa yuu tii mɨ́ang-láao.

ລາວ ມີ ຄອບຄົວ ຢູ່ ທີ່ ເມືອງລາວ.

He has a family in Laos.

19. A: kɔ̀i yàak dtɛng-ngáan gǎp jâo.

ຂ້ອຍ ຢາກ ແຕ່ງງານ ກັບ ເຈົ້າ.

I want to marry you.

B: láao yàak dtɛng-ngáan gǎp kón láao.

ລາວ ຢາກ ແຕ່ງງານ ກັບ ຄົນ ລາວ.

He wants to marry a Laotian.

20. A: kɔ̀i hak jâo lǎai.

ຂ້ອຍ ຮັກ ເຈົ້າ ຫລາຍ.

I love you very much.

B: láao hak kɔ̀ɔp-kúa lǎai.

ລາວ ຮັກ ຄອບຄົວ ຫລາຍ.

He loves his family very much.

C: kɔ̀i hak mɨ́ang-láao.

ຂ້ອຍ ຮັກ ເມືອງລາວ.

I love Laos.

Test 9

Match the English words with the Lao words.

A   Family

_____ 1. uncle   a. nɔ̂ɔng-sǎao ນ້ອງສາວ
_____ 2. grandfather   b. mia ເມຍ
_____ 3. daughter   c. lung ລຸງ
_____ 4. younger brother   d. lûuk-sǎao ລູກສາວ
_____ 5. grandmother   e. bpuu ປູ່
_____ 6. aunt   f. pǔa ຜົວ
_____ 7. son   g. âai ອ້າຍ
_____ 8. husband   h. lûuk-sáai ລູກຊາຍ
_____ 9. wife   i. mɛɛ ແມ່
_____ 10. older sister·   j. ûai ເອື້ອຍ
                                  k. nɔ̂ɔng-sáai ນ້ອງຊາຍ
                                  l. bpâa ປ້າ
                                  m. ñaa ຍ່າ

B   Occupations

_____ 1. dentist   a. nak-bìn ນັກບິນ
_____ 2. soldier   b. wit-sa-wa-gɔ̀ɔn ວິສະວະກອນ
_____ 3. nurse   c. pa-ñáa-bàan/náai-mɔ̌ɔ
                                     ພະຍາບານ/ນາຍໝໍ
_____ 4. farmer   d. nak-hían ນັກຮຽນ
_____ 5. movie star   e. dtàm-lùat ຕຳຫລວດ
_____ 6. police   f. nak-hɔ̂ɔng ນັກຮ້ອງ
_____ 7. student   g. dàa-láa ດາລາ
_____ 8. singer   h. mɔ̌ɔ-bpùa-kèo ໝໍປົວແຂ້ວ
_____ 9. engineer   i. àa-jàan ອາຈານ
_____ 10. pilot   j. ta-hǎan ທະຫານ
                                  k. nak-kían ນັກຽນ
                                  l. sáao-náa ຊາວນາ
                                  m. nak-tu-ra-gìt ນັກທຸລະກິດ

C   Animals

_____ 1. pig	a. nǔu ໝູ
_____ 2. fish	b. mâa ມ້າ
_____ 3. bird	c. kǎa ຊາ
_____ 4. horse	d. gai ໄກ່
_____ 5. monkey	e. sǔa ເສືອ
_____ 6. tiger	f. bpàa ປາ
_____ 7. dog	g. kwáai ຄວາຍ
_____ 8. shrimp	h. gûng ກຸ້ງ
_____ 9. elephant	i. mǎa ໝາ
_____ 10. buffalo	j. líng ລິງ
	k. mǔu ໝູ
	l. nok ນົກ
	m. sâang ຊ້າງ

Translate the following into English.

1. *A:* nɔ̂ɔng sáai jâo het wîak ñǎng.

ນ້ອງ ຊາຍ ເຈົ້າ ເຮັດ ວຽກ ຫຍັງ?

_____

2. láao dtɛng-ngáan gǎp kón ñii-bpun.

ລາວ ແຕ່ງງານ ກັບ ຄົນ ຍີ່ປຸ່ນ.

_____

3. *A:* bpèn ñǎng jâo jʉng bɔɔ mak àa-hǎan láao.

ເປັນ ຫຍັງ ເຈົ້າ ຈຶ່ງ ບໍ່ ມັກ ອາຫານ ລາວ?

_____

    B: prɔ-waa mán pět lǎai.

ເພາະ ວ່າ ມັນ ເຜັດ ຫລາຍ.

_____

4. tàa bɔɔ míi ngɔ́n gɔɔ ja gǎp mʉang-láao bɔɔ dâi.

ຖ້າ ບໍ່ ມີ ເງິນ ກໍ່ ຈະ ກັບ ເມືອງລາວ ບໍ່ ໄດ້.

_____

5. kɔ̀i kit waa láao míi kɔ̂ɔp-kúa lɛ́ɛo.

ຂ້ອຍ ຄິດ ວ່າ ລາວ ມີ ຄອບຄົວ ແລ້ວ.

_____

Punctuation Marks

1. ເຄື່ອງໝາຍຈ້ຳ ☐.☐ /kʉang-mǎai-jâm/ is used at the end of a sentence or paragraph like the full stop or period in English.

2. ເຄື່ອງໝາຍຈຸດ ☐,☐ /kʉang-mǎai-jǔt/ is used like the comma in English.

3. ເຄື່ອງໝາຍຈ້ຳຈຸດ ☐;☐ /kʉang-mǎai-jâm-jǔt/ is used like the semi-colon in English.

4. ເຄື່ອງໝາຍສອງຈ້ຳ ☐:☐ /kʉang-mǎai-sɔ̌ɔng-jâm/ is used like the colon in English.

5. ເຄື່ອງໝາຍຂິດຕໍ່ ☐-☐ /kʉang-mǎai-kìit-dtɔɔ/ is used like the dash in English.

6. ເຄື່ອງໝາຍຂິດກ້ອງ ☐___☐ /kʉang-mǎai-kìit-gɔ̂ng/ is used like the underline in English.

7. ເຄື່ອງໝາຍຈ້ຳໆ ☐ ... ☐ /kʉang-mǎai-jâm-jâm/ is used to show that there are more items that are not mentioned.

8. ເຄື່ອງໝາຍຖາມ ☐?☐ /kʉang-mǎai-tǎam/ is used like the question mark in English.

9. ເຄື່ອງໝາຍທ້ວງ ☐!☐ /kʉang-mǎai-tûang/ is used like the exclamation mark in English.

10. ເຄື່ອງໝາຍວົງຢືມ ☐" "☐ /kʉang-mǎai-wóng-yʉ̀ʉm/ is used like the quotation mark in English.

11. ເຄື່ອງໝາຍວົງເລັບ ☐( )☐ /kʉang-mǎai-wóng-lep/ is used like the parentheses in English.

12. ເຄື່ອງໝາຍລ້ຳ ☐ „ ☐ /kʉang-mǎai-lʉ̂m/ is used like the ditto mark in English.

13. ເຄື່ອງໝາຍ ແລະອື່ນໆ ⎡ຯລຯ⎤ /kʉang-mǎai-lɛ-ʉʉn-ʉʉn/ is used like the "etc," in English.

14. ເຄື່ອງໝາຍຊ້ຳ ⎡ໆ⎤ /kʉang-mǎai-sâm/ is used to indicate that the word or phrase is repeated for emphasis.

Other Symbols

ໄມ້ກັນ ◌ັ /mâi-gàn/ is the short vowel –ະ /ǎ/. It is written in this form when the syllable has a final consonant.

For example:

ກະ gǎ   ກັນ gàn

It is also used to change the long vowels ເ– (èe) and ແ– (ɛ̀ɛ) into the short vowels ເ–ະ (ě) and ແ–ະ (ɛ̌) when the syllable has a final consonant.

For example:

ເປນ bpèen   ເປັນ bpèn

ໄມ້ກົງ ◌ົ /mâi-gòng/ goes between two characters to form a short /o/ sound.

For example:

ໂຄນ kóon   ຄົນ kón

Reading Exercise

Read the following aloud and translate.

1. ເຈົ້າ ຊື່ ຫຍັງ?

2. ພາສາ ລາວ ບໍ່ ຍາກ.

3. ຂ້ອຍ ມັກ ສີຂາວ.

4. ລາວ ມີ ເຮືອນ ຫລັງ ງາມໆ.

5. ເຈົ້າ ສະບາຍ ດີບໍ່?

6. ຂ້ອຍ ເປັນ ຄົນລາວ.

7. ອັນນີ້ ລາຄາ ເທົ່າໃດ?

8. ທ່ານ ທານາກະ ເປັນ ຄົນຍີ່ປຸ່ນ.

9. ຫ້ອງນ້ຳ ຢູ່ໃສ?

10. ສໍ ຢູ່ ໃຕ້ ໂຕະ.

11. ໂຮງແຮມ ຢູ່ ທາງຂວາ.

12. ຄົນນັ້ນ ງາມ ອີ່ຫລີ.

13. ມື້ນີ້ ແມ່ນ ວັນຫຍັງ?

14. ມື້ນີ້ ແມ່ນ ວັນອາທິດ.

15. ລົດຢືນ ຂອງ ເຈົ້າ ສີຫຍັງ?

16. ຂ້ອຍ ໄປ ເຮັດວຽກ ຕອນເຊົ້າ.

17. ທ່ານ ສົມສຸກ ມັກ ເບິ່ງທິວີ/ໂທລະພາບ.

18. ພວກເຮົາ ຈະ ໄປ ກິນ ອາຫານລາວ.

19. ຄຸວນີ້ ເວລາ ເທົ່າໃດ?

20. ຈະ ໄປ ດື່ມ ເຫຼືອບິນ ຕອນ ສິບສອງໂມງ.

21. ເຈົ້າ ຈະ ໄປ ໃສ?

22. ຈະ ໄປ ຮຽນ ພາສາ ລາວ.

23. ຂ້ອຍ ບໍ່ ມັກ ອາຫານ ຈິນ.

24. ລາວ ມີ ໝາ ຢູ່ ເຮືອນ.

25. ຂ້ອຍ ຈະ ໄປ ເມືອງ ລາວ ເດືອນ ໜ້າ.

26. ວັນຈັນ ໜ້າ ຂ້ອຍ ຈະ ບໍ່ ຢູ່.

27. ພວກເຮົາ ຈະ ໄປ ຮຽນ ພາສາ ອັງກິດ ຢູ່ ທີ່
     ອາເມລິກາ.

28. ຄົນ ຍີ່ປຸ່ນ ມັກ ເຮັດ ວຽກ.

29. ຂ້ອຍ ຍາກ ເຊົ້າ ທ້ອງນ້ຳ.

30. ເຈົ້າ ກຳລັງ ເຮັດ ຫຍັງ?

31. ທ່ານ ຈອມ ປາກ ພາສາ ຈິນ ໄດ້.

32. ມີ້ນີ້ ເມື່ອຍ ອີ່ຫລີ.

33. ອັນນີ້ ແມ່ນ ໜ້າສີ ຂອງ ໃຜ?

34. ມື້ນີ້ ຮ້ອນ ຫລາຍ.

35. ຄິນຮັກ ເຈົ້າ ຢູ່ ຫຍັງ?

36. ຂ້ອຍ ອາບນ້ຳ ທຸກວັນ.

37. ຂ້ອຍ ຊັກ ເຄື່ອງນຸ່ງ ທຸກ ວັນເສົາ.

38. ເຮົາ ບໍ່ ຢາກ ຢູ່ ເຄື່ອງ ແພງ.

39. ຄຸວນີ້ ເຈັບ ຫົວ ຫລາຍ.

40. ຂ້ອຍ ຖຸ ແຂ້ວ ວັນ ລະ ສອງ ເທື່ອ.

Lesson 10

comparisons; adjectives; classifiers; practice reading
short sentences and paragraphs

bŏt-tii sĭp   ບົດທິ ສິບ   Lesson 10

kám-sǎp   ຄຳສັບ   Vocabulary

gwaa/gua ກວ່າ		than
tii-sŭt ທີ່ສຸດ		most
dtɛɛ ແຕ່		but
ñai ໃຫຍ່		big
nɔ̂i ນ້ອຍ		small
dtûi ຕຸ້ຍ		fat
jɔi ຈ່ອຍ		thin
nǎa ໜາ		thick
bàang ບາງ		thin
sǔung ສູງ		tall, high (height)
dîia/dtam ເຕ້ຍ/ຕ່ຳ		short (height)
dtàm ຕ່ຳ		low
ñáao ຍາວ		long (measurement)
sàn ສັ້ນ		short (measurement)
nǎk ໜັກ		heavy
bào ເບົາ		light (weight)
gwâang ກວ້າງ		wide
kɛ̂ɛp ແຄບ		narrow
hɔ̂ɔn ຮ້ອນ		hot
nǎao ໜາວ		cold (weather)
yen ເຢັນ		cold, cool
lǎai ຫລາຍ		much, many
nɔ̀i ໜ້ອຍ		little
gɛɛ/tào ແກ່/ເຖົ້າ		old
num/ɔɔn ໜຸ່ມ/ອ່ອນ		young
mai ໃໝ່		new

gao	ເກົ່າ	old
kĕng-héeng	ແຂງແຮງ	strong
ɔɔn-ɛ̀ɛ	ອ່ອນແອ	weak
sa-làat	ສະຫຼາດ	intelligent, smart
ngoo	ໂງ່	stupid
jêeng	ແຈ້ງ	light, clear
mʉ̀ʉt	ມືດ	dark
gài	ໄກ	far
gâi	ໃກ້	near
àn-dta-láai	ອັນຕະລາຍ	dangerous
bpɔ̀ɔt-pái	ປອດໄພ	safe
bpèn-dtàa-yâan	ເປັນຕາย້ານ	awful, terrifying, scary
bpèn-dtàa-sŏn-jài	ເປັນຕາສົນໃຈ	interesting
bpèn-dtàa-bʉa	ເປັນຕາເບື່ອ	boring
sa-dùak	ສະດວກ	convenient
sa-bàai	ສະບາຍ	comfortable
sa-àat	ສະອາດ	clean
bpʉ̂an	ເປື້ອນ	dirty
ñùng	ຫຍຸ້ງ	busy
waang/bpao	ຫວ່າງ/ເປົ່າ	free, empty
ka-ñăn	ຂະຫຍັນ	diligent
kîi-kâan	ຂີ້ຄ້ານ	lazy
hang-míi	ຮັ່ງມີ	rich
tuk/jòn	ທຸກ/ຈົນ	poor
ngáam	ງາມ	beautiful, pretty
bpèn-dtàa-hak	ເປັນຕາรัກ	cute
jâo-sûu	ເຈົ້າຊູ້	handsome
míi-sʉʉ-sĭang	ມີຊື່ສຽງ	famous
sămkán	ສำຄັນ	important
pi-sèet	ພິເສດ	special

kìi-tii ຂີ້ຕີ້	thrifty, cheap
dìi-jài ດີໃຈ	glad
jài-dìi ໃຈດີ	kind
jài-gwâang ໃຈກວ້າງ	generous
jài-yèn ໃຈເຢັນ	calm
jài-hɔ̂ɔn ໃຈຮ້ອນ	impatient
sua ຊົ່ວ	bad
ngîap/mit ງຽບ/ມິດ	quiet
kɔ̌ɔ ຂໍ	to ask for something
sùup ສູບ	to smoke
gìat-sáng/sáng ກຽດຊັງ/ຊັງ	to hate
kìi-dtǔa ຂີ້ຕົວະ	to lie
lôok ໂລກ	earth, world
láa-káa ລາຄາ	price
gàn ກັນ	each other
mǔan-gàn/kɯ̂ɯ gàn ເໝືອນກັນ/ຄືກັນ	same, to look like
kâai-kɯ̂ɯ-gàn ຄ້າຍຄືກັນ	to look like
tao-gàn/tao-gǎp ເທົ່າກັນ/ເທົ່າກັບ	equal

Other Helpful Nouns

nàa ໜ້າ	page
dtùa(dtòo)-nǎng-sɯ̌ɯ ຕົວ (ໂຕ) ໜັງສື	letter of the alphabet
dtuk-ga-dtàa ຕຸກກະຕາ	doll
yàa-sùup ຢາສູບ	cigarette
wáa-la-sǎan ວາລະສານ	magazine
mîit ມີດ	knife
tían ທຽນ	candle
kěm ເຂັມ	needle
ka-nǒm-òm ະຂົນົມອົມ	candy
gêɛo/jɔ̀ɔk-gêɛo ແກ້ວ/ຈອກແກ້ວ	glass

jɔ̀ɔk ຈອກ	cup
màak-mâi ໝາກໄມ້	fruit
màak-gûai ໝາກກ້ວຍ	banana
màak-muang ໝາກມ່ວງ	mango
màak-hung ໝາກຮຸ່ງ	papaya
màak-gìang ໝາກກ້ຽງ	orange
màak-pâao ໝາກພ້າວ	coconut
màak-móo ໝາກໂມ	watermelon
dɔ̀ɔk-mâi ດອກໄມ້	flower
dɔ̀ɔk-gù-làap ດອກກຸຫລາບ	rose
jàan ຈານ	plate
gɛ̂ɛo ແກ້ວ	bottle
hìip/gǎp ຫີບ/ກັບ	box
kai ໄຂ່	egg
kào-pǎt/kùa-kào ເຂົ້າຜັດ/ຂົ້ວເຂົ້າ	fried rice
ga-dàan ກະດານ	board
maak-baan ໝາກບານ	ball
jǒt-mǎai ຈົດໝາຍ	letter
èek-ga-sǎan ເອກະສານ	document
dtûu-yèn ຕູ້ເຢັນ	refrigerator
kɔ̂m-píu-dtɔ̂ɔ ຄອມພິວເຕີ	computer
buang ບ່ວງ	spoon
sɔm ສ້ອມ	fork
kán-hom ຄັນຮົ່ມ	umbrella
àa-káan/dtǔk ອາຄານ/ຕຶກ	building
kào-jii ເຂົ້າຈີ່	bread
sìin ຊີ້ນ	meat
ka-nǒm/kào nǒm ຂະໜົມ/ເຂົ້າໜົມ	cookie
sân ຊັ້ນ	floor, grade in school
sa-nit ຊະນິດ	kind (of things)

nâm-dtàan ນ້ຳຕານ	sugar
gừa ເກືອ	salt
fiim ຟິມ	film
tep/ga-sɛt ເທັບ/ກະແຊັກ	casette tape
wíi-dìi-òo ວິດີໂອ	video
sa-dtɛm ສະແຕມ	stamp
dàao ດາວ	star
dtàa wén/dùang-àa-tit ຕາເວັນ/ດວງອາທິດ	sun
dùang-jan/pa-jàn/dừan ດວງຈັນ/ພະຈັນ/ເດືອນ	moon
kɔ̌ɔng-kwǎn ຂອງຂວັນ	present
ta-nǒn ຖະໜົນ	road
táang-lot-fái ທາງລົດໄຟ	railway
kɔ̌ɔng/hɔng ຄອງ/ຮ່ອງ	canal
sǐi-nêe/hǔup-ngáo/nǎng ຊີເນ/ຮູບເງົາ/ໜັງ	movie
lừang ເລື້ອງ	story

lak-sǎ-na-náam ລັກສະນະນາມ Classifiers

Classifiers are words which are required in Lao when counting or referring to any concrete noun.

English has similar words. When we say "three glasses of water," "one sheet of paper," "eight head of cattle," the words "glasses," "sheet" and "head" could be called classifiers. Lao, however, uses classifiers much more often than English. It is impossible to speak acceptable Lao without mastering the use of classifiers.

A classifier is generally used with a category of nouns perceived to have a common characteristic. These categories often seem arbitrary. Therefore, it is a good idea to memorize the classifier along with the noun when learning new vocabulary.

Common Classifiers

1. kón (ຄົນ) » people.
2. dtùa/dtòo (ຕົວ/ໂຕ) » animals, shirts, costumes, letters of the
   alphabet, dolls, etc.
3. lèm (ເຫຼັ້ມ) » candles, books.
4. hŭa (ຫົວ) » books, notebooks, magazines, heads of cabbage,
   heads of garlic, etc.
5. àn (ອັນ) » pieces of candy, ashtrays, round objects,
   objects with unknown classifiers, stamps.
6. jɔ̀ɔk (ຈອກ) » glasses, cups, numbers of glasses of beer, cups
   of tea, coffe, water, etc.
7. pɛn (ແຜ່ນ) » boards, pieces of paper, pieces of corrugated
   metal, pieces of flat objects.
8. nuai (ໜ່ວຍ) » fruits, mountains, balls and other round things,
   radios, TVs, refrigerators, computers, electrical or
   mechanical machines, clocks, watches, tables, chairs,
   beds.
9. sa-bǎp (ສະບັບ) » newspapers, letters, documents.
10. lám (ລຳ) » ships, boats, airplanes, pieces of wood, sticks of
    bamboo.
11. kán (ຄັນ) » cars, motorcycles, bicycles, umbrellas, fishing
    rods.
12. gâan (ກ້ານ) » spoons, forks, pens, letters.
13. lăng (ຫຼັງ) » houses, buildings, hospitals.
14. gɔ̂ɔn (ກ້ອນ) » pieces of bread, pieces of meat, cookies,
    bars of soap, sugar cubes, pieces of candy, etc.
15. dtɔn (ຕ່ອນ) » pieces of meat, pieces of cloth.
16. chân (ຊັ້ນ) » floors of buildings, grades or classes in
    schools, classes of train or airplane seats.

17. hɔ̀ng (ຫ້ອງ) » rooms.

18. dɔ̀ɔk (ດອກ) » flowers, lamps, nails.

19. kâng/tɯa (ຄັ້ງ/ເທື່ອ) » times (numbers of occurrences).

20. yàang (ຢ່າງ) » kinds of things, numbers of things.

21. bɔn (ບ່ອນ) » numbers of seats.

22. tùai (ຖ້ວຍ) » numbers of cups of soup, etc.

23. kùat (ຂວດ) » numbers of bottles of beer, water, etc.

24. jàan (ຈານ) » numbers of plates of rice, dishes, food, etc.

25. sèn (ເສັ້ນ) » threads, neckties, tires, necklaces,
     bracelets, roads, hairs, pieces of chalk, railways.

26. gɔ̀ɔk (ກອກ) » cigarettes.

27. mûan (ມ້ວນ) » rolls of film, casette tapes, video tapes.

28. dùang (ດວງ) » stars, suns, moons, knives, needles.

29. hɔɔ (ຫໍ) » presents, bags of sweets, bags of snacks,
     wrapped things.

30. sǎai (ສາຍ) » rivers, canals.

31. kuu (ຄູ່) » pairs of things or people.

32. sut (ຊຸດ) » sets of things, suits, dresses.

33. lɯang (ເລື່ອງ) » movies, plays, stories, subjects.

34. dtôn (ຕົ້ນ) » trees.

35. gɔ̂ɔ (ກໍ້) » rolls of film, small and round objects.

How to Use Classifiers

1. noun + cardinal number + classifier

   (one, two, three, ... nɯng, sɔ̌ɔng, sǎam)

   e.g. mǎa sǎam dtɒ̀ɒ = three dogs

   kɔ̀i mɨi mǎa sǎam dtɒ̀ɒ. = I have three dogs.

   bpûm hâa hǔa = five books

   bpûm hâa hǔa yùu tǎng dtó.

   = Five books are on the table.

   nɯng is usually replaced with dìao (กู่ง) in normal speech and dìao is placed after the classifier.

   e.g.   mǎa nɯng dtɒ̀ɒ = mǎa dtɒ̀ɒ dìao (one dog)

2. noun + classifier + nîi, nân (or hàn) or pûun (or pûn)

   e.g. mǎa dtɒ̀ɒ nîi = this dog

   mǎa dtɒ̀ɒ nîi ngáam. = This dog is beautiful.

   bpûm hǔa nân = that book

   bpûm hǔa nân tao-dǎi? = How much is that book?

3. noun + classifier + ordinal number

   (first, second, third, ... (ที่) tîi nɯng, tîi sɔ̌ɔng, tîi sǎam)

   e.g. mǎa dtɒ̀ɒ tîi nɯng = the first dog

   mǎa dtɒ̀ɒ tîi nɯng sǐi dàm. = The first dog is black.

   bpûm hǔa tîi sɔ̌ɔng = the second book

   bpûm hǔa tîi sɔ̌ɔng yùu tǎng dtó.

   = The second book is on the table.

   tîi nɯng is sometimes replaced with lɛ̂ɛk (แรก) or tám-ìt (ทำอิก) in normal speech.

   e.g.   bpûm hǔa tîi nɯng = bpûm hǔa lɛ̂ɛk (the first book)

4. noun + jǎk + <u>classifier</u>
    (asking for the number or amount of something)
    e.g. mǎa jǎk <u>dtòo</u>? = how many dogs?
    jâo mîi mǎa jǎk <u>dtòo</u>.
        = How many dogs do you have?
    bpûm jǎk <u>hǔa</u>. = how many books?
    láao aan bpûm jǎk <u>hǔa</u>.
        = How many books did he read?

5. noun + <u>classifier</u> + adjective
    e.g. mǎa <u>dtòo</u> mai = a new dog
    kòi mîi mǎa <u>dtòo</u> mai. = I have a new dog.
    bpûm <u>hǔa</u> gao = an old book
    nîi mɛɛn bpûm <u>hǔa</u> gao. = This is an old book.

6. noun + <u>classifier</u> + dǎi = which one.
    e.g. mǎa <u>dtòo</u> dǎi. = Which dog?
    jâo mak mǎa <u>dtòo</u> dǎi tîi sùt.
        = Which dog do you like most?
    bpûm <u>hǔa</u> dǎi. = Which book?
    bpûm <u>hǔa</u> dǎi kɔ̌ɔng jâo.
        = Which one is your book?

7. (noun) + lǎai (ຫລາຍ) + <u>classifier</u> = many _____
    e.g. mǎa lǎai <u>dtòo</u> or lǎai dtòo = many dogs

Note: When a noun is understood from the context, it is often omitted.
    e.g.   hàa <u>hǔa</u> = five books
    <u>hǔa</u> nîi = this book
    <u>hǔa</u> lɛ̂ɛk = the first book
    jǎk <u>hǔa</u> = how many books?
    <u>hǔa</u> gao = an old book
    <u>hǔa</u> dǎi = which book?

Conversation

John: ga-bpǎo nuai nân láa-káa tao-dǎi.

ຈອມ: ກະເປົ໋າ   ໜ່ວຍ   ນັ້ນ   ລາຄາ   ເທົ່າໃດ?

How much is that bag?

Konkǎai-kɯang: hàa hɔ̀ɔi gìip.

ຄົນຂາຍເຄື່ອງ: ຫ້າ   ຮ້ອຍ   ກີບ.

It's five hundred kip.

John: nuai nîi děe.

ຈອມ: ໜ່ວຍ   ນີ້   ເດ?

What about this one?

Konkǎai-kɯang: àn-nân sǎam hɔ̀ɔi hàa sǐp.

ຄົນຂາຍເຄື່ອງ: ອັນນັ້ນ   ສາມ   ຮ້ອຍ   ຫ້າ   ສິບ.

That one is three hundred and fifty.

John: jâo míi jǎk sǐi.

ຈອມ: ເຈົ້າ   ມີ   ຈັກ   ສີ?

How many colors do you have?

Konkǎai-kɯang: míi lǎai sǐi.

ຄົນຂາຍເຄື່ອງ: ມີ   ຫຼາຍ   ສີ.

Many colors.

jâo mak sǐi ñǎng lǎai tii-sǔt.

ເຈົ້າ   ມັກ   ສີ   ຫຍັງ   ຫຼາຍ   ທີ່ສຸດ?

What color do you like the most?

John: kɔ̀i mak sǐi dàm lǎai tii sǔt.

ຈອມ: ຂ້ອຍ   ມັກ   ສີ   ດຳ   ຫຼາຍ   ທີ່   ສຸດ.

I like black the most.

kɔ̀i kɔ̌ɔ bəng nuai sǐi dàm gǎp sǐi kàao nân dɛɛ.

ຂ້ອຍ ຂໍ ເບິ່ງ ໜ່ວຍ ສີ ດຳ ກັບ ສີ ຂາວ ນັ້ນ ແດ່?

May I see the black and the white ones?

Konkǎai-kʉang: nîi dee.*

ຄົນຂາຍເຄື່ອງ: ນີ້ ເດ.

    Here you are.

John: kɔ̀i kit waa kɔ̀i mak nuai sǐi dàm lǎai gwaa.

ຈອມ: ຂ້ອຍ ຄິດ ວ່າ ຂ້ອຍ ມັກ ໜ່ວຍ ສີ ດຳ ຫລາຍ ກວ່າ.

    I think I like black better.

    láa-káa tao-dǎi gɔ̌.

      ລາຄາ   ເທົ່າໃດ ກໍ?

    How much is it again?

Konkǎai-kʉang: hàa hɔ̂ɔi.

ຄົນຂາຍເຄື່ອງ: ຫ້າ ຮ້ອຍ.

    Five hundred.

John: sii hɔ̂ɔi dâi bɔɔ

ຈອມ: ສີ່ ຮ້ອຍ ໄດ້ ບໍ?

    Can you make it four hundred?

Konkǎai: bɔɔ dâi dɔ̀ɔk.* ào sii hɔ̂ɔi hàa sǐp sǎa.*

ຄົນຂາຍເຄື່ອງ: ບໍ່ ໄດ້ ດອກ.   ເອົາ ສີ່ ຮ້ອຍ ຫ້າ ສິບ ຊ້າ.

    No, I can't. Let's make it four hundred and fifty.

John: dtǒk-lóng.

ຈອມ: ຕົກລົງ.

    O.K.

*ending particles used for emphasis

bpà-ñòok   ປະໂຫຍກ   **Sentences**

1. A: láao sǔung gwàa kɔ̀i.

   ລາວ ສູງ ກວ່າ ຂ້ອຍ.

   He is taller than I.

   B: bpûm hǔa nîi péeng gwaa hǔa nân.

   ບຶ້ມ ຫົວ ນີ້ ແພງ ກວ່າ ຫົວ ນັ້ນ.

   This book is more expensive than that one.

   C: hǔa nîi dìi gwaa.

   ຫົວ ນີ້ ດີ ກວ່າ.

   This one is better.

   D: hǔa nân ngáam gwaa.

   ຫົວ ນັ້ນ ງາມ ກວ່າ.

   That one is more beautiful.

2. A: láao sǔung tii-sǔt nái hɔ̀ng.

   ລາວ ສູງ ທີ່ສຸດ ໃນ ຫ້ອງ.

   He is the tallest in the room.

   B: bpûm hǔa nîi péeng tii-sǔt.

   ບຶ້ມ ຫົວ ນີ້ ແພງ ທີ່ສຸດ.

   This book is the most expensive.

   C: àn-nîi dìi tii-sǔt.

   ອັນນີ້ ດີ ທີ່ ສຸດ.

   This is the best.

   D: àn-nân ngáam tii-sǔt.

   ອັນນັ້ນ ງາມ ທີ່ສຸດ.

   That one is the most beautiful.

3. A: láao gǎp jâo mɛɛn* pǎi sǔung gwaa gàn.

   ລາວ ກັບ ເຈົ້າ ແມ່ນ ໃຜ ສູງ ກວ່າ ກັນ?

   Who is taller between him and you?

   *mɛɛn is often used in front of question words for emphasis.

B: láao sǔung gwaa (kɔ̀i).

ລາວ   ສູງ ກວ່າ (ຂ້ອຍ).

He is taller (than I).

A: bpûm hǔa nîi gǎp hǔa nân,

ປຶ້ມ   ຫົວ ນີ້ ກັບ ຫົວ ນັ້ນ,

àn dǎi pɛ́ɛng gwaa gàn.

ອັນ ໃດ ແພງ ກວ່າ ກັນ?

Between this book and that book,

which one is more expensive?

B: bpûm hǔa nîi pɛ́ɛng gwaa (hǔa nân).

ປຶ້ມ   ຫົວ ນີ້ ແພງ ກວ່າ   (ຫົວ ນັ້ນ).

This book is more expensive (than that one).

A: àn-dǎi dìi gwaa.

ອັນໃດ ດີ ກວ່າ?

Which one is better?

B: àn-nîi dìi gwaa.

ອັນນີ້ ດີ ກວ່າ.

This one is better.

A: àn-dǎi ngáam gwaa.

ອັນໃດ ງາມ ກວ່າ?

Which one is more beautiful?

B: àn-nân ngáam gwaa.

ອັນນັ້ນ ງາມ ກວ່າ.

That one is more beautiful.

4. A: A ñai gwaa B, dtɛɛ C ñai tii-sǔt.

A ໃຫຍ່ ກວ່າ B, ແຕ່ C ໃຫຍ່ ທີ່ສຸດ.

A is bigger than B, but C is the biggest.

B: kɔ̀i mak sǐi kǎao lǎai gwaa sǐi dàm,

ຂ້ອຍ ມັກ ສີ ຂາວ ຫລາຍ ກວ່າ ສີ ດຳ.

dtɛɛ kɔ̀i mak sǐi fâa lǎai tii sǔt.

ແຕ່ ຂ້ອຍ ມັກ ສີ ຟ້າ ຫລາຍ ທີ່ສຸດ.

I like white more than black, but I like blue the most.

5. A: húa-bìn lám nîi ñai tii-sǔt nái lôok.
       ເຮືອບິນ ລຳ ນີ້ ໃຫຍ່ ທີ່ສຸດ ໃນ ໂລກ.
       This airplane is the biggest in the world.

   B: kɔ̀i sǔung tii-sǔt nái húan.
       ຂ້ອຍ ສູງ ທີ່ສຸດ ໃນ ເຮືອນ.
       I am the tallest in the house.

   C: láao hang-míi tii-sǔt nái múang-láao.
       ລາວ ຮັ່ງມີ ທີ່ສຸດ ໃນ ເມືອງລາວ.
       He is the richest in Laos.

6. A: àn-nîi gǎp àn-nân kúu-gàn.
       ອັນນີ້ ກັບ ອັນນັ້ນ ຄືກັນ.
       This one and that one are the same.
       (Literally: This one and that one look like each other.)

   B: sɔ̌ɔng kón nân bəng kâai-kúu-gàn.
       ສອງ ຄົນ ນັ້ນ ເບິ່ງ ຄ້າຍຄືກັນ.
       Those two people look alike.

   C: bpûm sɔ̌ɔng hǔa nîi láa-káa tao-gàn.
       ປຶ້ມ ສອງ ຫົວ ນີ້ ລາຄາ ເທົ່າກັນ.
       The price of these two books is the same.

7. kǎo-jâo hak gàn lǎai.
    ເຂົາເຈົ້າ ຮັກ ກັນ ຫຼາຍ.
    They love each other very much.

8. láao sáng jâo ñɔ̌ɔn waa jâo mak kìi-dtǔa.
    ລາວ ຊັງ ເຈົ້າ ຍ້ອນ ວ່າ ເຈົ້າ ມັກ ຂີ້ຕົວະ.
    He hates you because you often lie.
    (Literally: ... because you like to lie.)

9. A: húan jâo míi sǎt-líang bɔɔ?
       ເຮືອນ ເຈົ້າ ມີ ສັດລ້ຽງ ບໍ່?
       Do you have pets at home?

   B: míi. míi mɛ́ɛo sɔ̌ɔng dtòo.
       ມີ. ມີ ແມວ ສອງ ໂຕ.
       Yes. I have two cats.

The following sentences demonstrate how to use different classifiers. The underlined words are classifiers.

10. míi kón hàa <u>kón</u> yuu nái hɔ̀ng.

ມີ ຄົນ ຫ້າ <u>ຄົນ</u> ຢູ່ ໃນ ຫ້ອງ.

There are five people in the room.

11. sʉ̀a <u>dtòo</u> nîi bɔɔ péɛng.

ເສື້ອ <u>ໂຕ</u> ນີ້ ບໍ່ ແພງ.

This shirt is not expensive.

12. pǎi kǐan bpʉ̂m <u>hǔa</u> nân.

ໃຜ ຂຽນ ປຶ້ມ <u>ຫົວ</u> ນັ້ນ?

Who wrote that book?

13. jâo mak <u>àn</u> dǎi lǎai tii-sǔt.

ເຈົ້າ ມັກ <u>ອັນ</u> ໃດ ຫລາຍ ທີ່ສຸດ?

Which one do you like the best?

14. hìip <u>nuai</u> nîi bɔɔ kɔi dìi.

ຫີບ <u>ຫນ່ວຍ</u> ນີ້ ບໍ່ ຄ່ອຍ ດີ.

This bag is not very good.

15. jîa <u>pɛn</u> nân bàang lǎai.

ເຈ້ຍ <u>ແຜ່ນ</u> ນັ້ນ ບາງ ຫລາຍ.

This piece of paper is very thin.

16. mʉ̂ʉ-nîi kɔi gìn màak-gûai sɔ̌ɔng <u>nuai</u>.

ມື້ນີ້ ຂ້ອຍ ກິນ ຫມາກກ້ວຍ ສອງ <u>ຫນ່ວຍ</u>.

Today I ate two bananas.

17. mʉ̂ʉ-wáan-nîi jâo aan nǎng-sʉ̌ʉ-pím jak <u>sa-bǎp</u>.

ມື້ວານນີ້ ເຈົ້າ ອ່ານ ຫນັງສືພິມ ຈັກ <u>ສະບັບ</u>?

How many newspapers did you read yesterday?

18. kɔi míi tóo-la-tat sǎam <u>nuai</u>, kɔm-píu-dtɔ̂ə <u>nuai</u> nʉng.

ຂ້ອຍ ມີ ໂທລະທັດ ສາມ <u>ຫນ່ວຍ</u>, ຄອມພິວເຕີ <u>ຫນ່ວຍ</u> ນຶ່ງ.

I have three televisions and one computer.

19. hʉ̌a-bìn <u>lám</u> nîi máa jàak wíang-jàn.

ເຮືອບິນ <u>ລຳ</u> ນີ້ ມາ ຈາກ ວຽງຈັນ.

This airplane came from Vientiane.

20. lot kán nîi het jàak ñii-bpun.

ລົດ ຄັນ ນີ້ ເຣັດ ຈາກ ຍີ່ປຸ່ນ.

This car is made in Japan.

21. kòi sûu húan lǎng mai.

ຂ້ອຍ ຊື້ ເຮືອນ ຫລັງ ໃໝ່.

I bought a new house.

22. sîin núa dtɔn níi sêɛp ii-lîi.

ຊິ້ນ ງົວ ຕ່ອນ ນີ້ ແຊບ ອີ່ຫລີ.

This piece of meat is really delicious.

23. kòi yuu sân tii sǎam.

ຂ້ອຍ ຢູ່ ຊັ້ນ ທີ ສາມ.

I live on the third floor.

24. húan láao míi hɔ̀ng-nɔ́ɔn sii hɔ̀ng.

ເຮືອນ ລາວ ມີ ຫ້ອງນອນ ສີ່ ຫ້ອງ.

His house has four bedrooms.

25. dɔ́ɔk-mâi dɔ̀ɔk nîi ngáam lǎai.

ດອກໄມ້ ດອກ ນີ້ ງາມ ຫລາຍ.

This flower is very beautiful.

26. kòi kɔ́əi bpài múang láao hàa tɯa.

ຂ້ອຍ ເຄີຍ ໄປ ເມືອງ ລາວ ຫ້າ ເທື່ອ.

I have been to Laos five times.

27. yuu tɤ́ng dto míi àa-hǎan hǒk yɯang .

ຢູ່ ເທິງ ໂຕະ ມີ ອາຫານ ຫົກ ເຍື່ອງ .

There are five kinds of food on the table.

28. kɔ̌ɔ kào nɯng jàan.

ຂໍ ເຂົ້າ ນຶ່ງ ຈານ.

Give me one (plate of) rice.

29. kɔ̌ɔ nâm yèn sɔ̌ɔng jɔ̀ɔk.

ຂໍ ນ້ຳ ເຢັນ ສອງ ຈອກ.

Give me two glasses of cold water.

30.   kɔ̌ɔ gàa-fée hɔ̂ɔn sǎam jɔ̀ɔk.

ຂໍ   ກາເຟ   ຮ້ອນ   ສາມ   <u>ຈອກ</u>.

Give me three cups of hot coffee.

31.   ào bìa sii gɛ́ɛo.

ເອົາ ເບຍ ສີ່   <u>ແກ້ວ</u>.

I want four bottles of beer.

32.   ào kâo-pǎt hàa jàan.

ເອົາ ເຂົ້າຜັດ ຫ້າ <u>ຈານ</u>.

I want five plates of fried rice.

33.   ào nâm-dtàan hǒk gɔ̂ɔn.

ເອົາ   ນ້ຳຕານ   ຫົກ   <u>ກ້ອນ</u>.

I want six cubes of sugar.

34. A: jâo míi bpàak-gàa jǎk gâan.

ເຈົ້າ ມີ ປາກກາ   ຈັກ <u>ກ້ານ</u>?

How many pens do you have?

B: míi sɔ̌ɔng gâan.

ມີ ສອງ <u>ກ້ານ</u>.

I have two.

A: jâo míi sɔ̌ɔ jǎk sèn.

ເຈົ້າ ມີ ສໍ ຈັກ <u>ເສັ້ນ</u>?

How many pencils do you have?

B: míi sèn dìao.

ມີ <u>ເສັ້ນ</u> ດຽວ.

I have one.

35.   sɔ̀i <u>sèn</u> nìi láa-káa tâo-dǎi.

ສ້ອຍ <u>ເສັ້ນ</u> ນີ້   ລາຄາ ເທົ່າໃດ?

How much is this necklace?

36.   láao sùup-yàa mùu la sǐp gɔ̀ɔk.

ລາວ   ສູບຢາ ມື້ ລະ ສິບ <u>ກອກ</u>.

He smokes ten cigarettes a day.

37.   pûak-háo gàm-láng bɔng wíi-đii-ɔ̀o mûan tii sǎam yuu.

ພວກເຮົາ   ກຳລັງ   ເບິ່ງ   ວິດີໂອ   ມ້ວນ ທີ ສາມ ຢູ່.

We are watching the third video.

38.   kɔ̀i sน̂น sa-dtɛ̀m sáao àn.

ຂ້ອຍ ຊື້ ສະແຕມ ຊາວ ອັນ.

I bought twenty stamps.

39.   láao dâi móong nuai mai.

ລາວ ໄດ້   ໂມງ ໜ່ວຍ ໃໝ່.

He has a new watch.

40.   mɛɛ sน̂น kào-nǒm sii hɔɔ.

ແມ່ ຊື້ ເຂົ້າໜົມ ສີ່ ຫໍ່.

Mother bought four packages of snacks.

41.   mɛɛ-nâm lám nîi ñáao lǎai.

ແມ່ນ້ຳ   ລຳ ນີ້ ຍາວ ຫລາຍ.

This river is very long.

42.   gɔɔp kuu nân ngáam tii-sùt.

ເກີບ   ຄູ່ ນັ້ນ ງາມ   ທີ່ສຸດ.

That pair of shoes is the prettiest.

43.   bpน̂m sut nîi bpèn-dtàa-sǒn-jài.

ປຶ້ມ ຊຸດ ນີ້   ເປັນຕາສົນໃຈ.

This set of books is interesting.

44.   kน́น-wáan-nîi kɔ̀i bɔng hน̂up-ngáo sǎam lน̆ang.

ຄືນວານນີ້   ຂ້ອຍ ເບິ່ງ   ຮູບເງົາ   ສາມ ເລື້ອງ.

Last night I watched three movies.

45.   dtôn mâi dtôn nân àa-ñu lǎai gwàa pán bpìi.

ຕົ້ນໄມ້   ຕົ້ນ ນັ້ນ   ອາຍຸ ຫລາຍ ກວ່າ ພັນ ປີ.

That tree is more than a thousand years old.

Test 10

Matching

A   Adjectives

_____ 1. tall   a. nɔ̌ɔi   ນ້ອຍ
_____ 2. new   b. gài   ໄກ
_____ 3. fat   c. sǔung   ສູງ
_____ 4. cold   d. nǎk   ໜັກ
_____ 5. intelligent   e. nǎao   ໜາວ
_____ 6. small   f. ñùng   ຫຍຸ້ງ
_____ 7. far   g. pi-sèet   ພິເສດ
_____ 8. busy   h. hang-míi   ຮັ່ງມີ
_____ 9. rich   i. dtùi   ຕຸ້ຍ
_____ 10. special   j. gâi   ໃກ້
                           k. sa-làat   ສະຫລາດ
                           l. mai   ໃໝ່
                           m. tuk/jòn   ທຸກ/ຈົນ

B   Nouns

_____ 1. cigarette   a. hûup-ngáo   ຮູບເງົາ
_____ 2. magazine   b. kùat   ຂວດ
_____ 3. letter   c. jàan   ຈານ
_____ 4. meat   d. sîin   ຊີ້ນ
_____ 5. plate   e. jŏt-mǎai   ຈົດໝາຍ
_____ 6. sugar   f. àa-káan/dtǔk   ອາຄານ/ຕຶກ
_____ 7. movie   g. dàao   ດາວ
_____ 8. story   h. wáa-la-sǎan
                              ວາລະສານ
_____ 9. building   i. gùa   ເກືອ
_____ 10. star   j. lɯang   ເລື່ອງ
                           k. yàa-sùup   ຢາສູບ
                           l. buang   ບ່ວງ
                           m. nâam-dtàan   ນ້ຳຕານ

C   Classifiers

Match the following nouns with their proper classifiers.

_____ 1. mǎa ໝາ   a. kùat ຂວດ

_____ 2. lot-ñón ລົດຍົນ   b. tɛng ແຫ່ງ

_____ 3. nǎng-sǔu-pím ໜັງສືພິມ   c. gâan ກ້ານ

_____ 4. hʉa-bìn ເຮືອບິນ   d. kán ຄັນ

_____ 5. bìa ເບຍ   e. nuai ໜ່ວຍ

_____ 6. hʉan ເຮືອນ   f. sèn ເສັ້ນ

_____ 7. tíi-wíi ທີວີ   g. dtùa ຕົວ

_____ 8. sɔ̌ɔ-dàm ສໍດຳ   h. lám ລຳ

_____ 9. jia ເຈັ້ຍ   j. sa-bǎp ສະບັບ

_____ 10. ta-nǒn ຖະໜົນ   k. pɛn/bài ແຜ່ນ/ໃບ

                                     l. lǎng ຫລັງ

                                     m. àn ອັນ

Translate the following into English.

1. A: màak-muang nuai   dăi sêɛp tii-sŭt.
    ໝາກມ່ວງ   ໜ່ວຍ   ໃດ ແຊບ ທີ່ສຸດ?

    B: kit waa nuai nîi sêɛp tii-sŭt.
    ຄິດ ວ່າ   ໜ່ວຍ ນີ້ ແຊບ   ທີ່ສຸດ.

2. A: hŭan jâo míi jăk sân.   B: míi săam sân.
    ເຮືອນ ເຈົ້າ ມີ ຈັກ ຊັ້ນ?   ມີ   ສາມ   ຊັ້ນ.

3. A: hŭa lám lêɛk jà máa mɯa-dăi.
    ເຮືອ ລຳ   ແລກ ຈະ ມາ ເມື່ອໃດ?

    B: jà máa mɯ̂ɯ-ɯɯn.
    ຈະ ມາ   ມື້ອື່ນ.

4. mɯ̂ɯ-wáan-níi sɯ̂ɯ moóng nuai mai.
    ມື້ວານນີ້   ຊື້   ໂມງ ໜ່ວຍ ໃໝ່.

5. tii sŭan-săt míi sâang hăa dtoo.
    ທີ່ ສວນສັດ ມີ   ຊ້າງ   ຫ້າ   ໂຕ.

Reading Exercise

Read the following sentences aloud and translate.

1. ອາເມລິກາ ໃຫຍ່ ກວ່າ ເມືອງ ລາວ .

2. ລົດ ຄັນ ນັ້ນ ງາມ ທີ່ສຸດ .

3. ຂ້ອຍ ມັກ ສີ ຂາວ ຫລາຍ ກວ່າ ສີ ດຳ .

4. ລາວ ມີ ໝາ ສາມ ໂຕ .

5. ລູກຊາຍ ຂ້ອຍ ຢາກ ເປັນ ນັກບິນ .

6. ເຈົ້າ ມີ ພີ່ນ້ອງ ຈັກ ຄົນ?

7. ເອື້ອຍ ເຈົ້າ ເຮັດ ວຽກ ຫຍັງ?

8. ເປັນຫຍັງ ຄົນ ຍີ່ປຸ່ນ ຈຶ່ງ ມັກ ເຮັດ ວຽກ?

9. ຂ້ອຍ ຢາກ ຈະ ມີ ລູກ ສອງ ຄົນ .

10. ມີຄວາມນີ້ ຂ້ອຍ ຊື້ ເກີບ ສອງ ຄູ່ .

11. ທ້າວ ສອນ ເວົ້າ ພາສາ ອັງກິດ ບໍ່ ຄ່ອຍ ຖຶກ .

12. ເປັນຫຍັງ ເຈົ້າ ຈຶ່ງ ບໍ່ ໄປ ເຮັດ ວຽກ?

13. ເຈົ້າ ອາຍຸ ເທົ່າໃດ?

14. ຂ້ອຍ ເປັນ ນັກທຸລະກິດ .

15. ລາວ ມີ ຄົນຮັກ ຫລາຍ ຄົນ .

16. ຂ້ອຍ ກຳລັງ ແຕ່ງໂຕ .

17. ຂ້ອຍ ຊຸກ ເຄື່ອງມຸ່ງ ທຸກມື້.

18. ມື້ອື່ນ ຂ້ອຍ ຈະ ໄປ ຕັດ ຜົມ.

19. ຂ້ອຍ ມີ ວຽກ ຫລາຍ ອິຫລີ.

20. ຖ້າ ເຈົ້າ ມີ ເງິນ ຫລາຍໆ ເຈົ້າ ຈະ ເຮັດ ຫຍັງ?

21. ມື້ນີ້ ຂ້ອຍ ບໍ່ ຄ່ອຍ ສະບາຍ.

22. ມື້ອື່ນ ຂ້ອຍ ໄປ ຫລິ້ນ ບໍ່ ໄດ້.

23. ຣຽນ ພາສາ ລາວ ມ່ວນ ຫລາຍ.

24. ຜູ້ຊາຍ ຄົນ ນັ້ນ ມັກ ອ່ານ ຫັງສື.

25. ຫ້ອງນໍ້າ ຜູ້ຍິງ ຍູ່ໃສ?

26. ທ່ານ ຄຳ ຍູ່ ຫ້ນ ສອງ.

27. ຂ້ອຍ ມັກ ອ່ານ ຫັງສືພິມ ພາສາ ອັງກິດ.

28. ດຽວນີ້ ລາວ ບໍ່ຄ່ອຍ ໄປ ຣຽນ ພາສາລາວ ຍູ່ ວັດ.

29. ຮ້ານອາຫານ ຍູ່ໃກ້ ກັບ ໂຮງແຮມ ວັງວຽງ.

30. ຂ້ອຍ ຍາກ ເຂົ້າ ຫລາຍ ເພາະວ່າ ຂ້ອຍ ບໍ່ ໄດ້ ກິນ ເຂົ້າເຊົ້າ.

31. ເປັນຫຍັງ ຄົນນັ້ນ ຈຶ່ງ ບໍ່ ຍາກ ໄປທ່ຽວ ກັບ ເຮົາ.

32. ລາວ ບອກວ່າ ກິນ ບໍ່ ໄດ້ ເພາະວ່າ ມັນ ເຜັດ ຫລາຍໂພດ.

33. ນ້ອງຊາຍ ຂ້ອຍ ບໍ່ມັກ ອ່ານ ໜັງສືພິມ ແຕ່ ລາວ
    ມັກ ເບິ່ງ ໂທລະພາບ.

34. ລາວ ເປັນ ນັກ ທຸລະກິດ ທີ່ ເກັ່ງ ອິຫລິ.

35. ເຮືອນ ຫລັງ ນີ້ ກັບ ຫລັງ ນັ້ນ ຫລັງ ໃດ ງາມ
    ກວ່າກັນ.

36. ເຮືອນ ເຈົ້າ ມີ ສັດລ້ຽງ ບໍ່?

37. ເຮົາ ຂາຍ ອາຫານ ຢູ່ທີ່ ເມືອງ ແຂວງເຂ, ສະຫະລັດ
    ອາເມລິກາ.

38. ອາທິດ ທີ່ແລ້ວ ເຮົາ ໄປ ຫລິ້ນ ສວນສັດ.

39. ຄອບຄົວ ຂອງ ຂ້ອຍ ມີ ຫ້າ ຄົນ.

40. ທ່ານ ພອນ ເປັນ ພະນັກງານລັດ ທີ່ ເມືອງ ລາວ.

Read the following paragraphs aloud and translate.

ຄອບຄົວຂອງຂ້ອຍແມ່ນຄອບຄົວໃຫຍ່ . ໃນເຮືອນຂ້ອຍມີທັງໝົດ
ແປດຄົນ . ມີພໍ່, ແມ່, ເອື້ອຍ 2 ຄົນ, ອ້າຍ 1 ຄົນ,
ນ້ອຍຊາຍ 1 ຄົນ, ນ້ອງສາວ 1 ຄົນ ແລະໂຕຂ້ອຍ . ພໍ່ຂອງ
ຂ້ອຍເປັນຊາວນາ . ແມ່ຂອງຂ້ອຍເປັນແມ່ເຮືອນ . ພວກເຮົາບໍ່ມີ
ເງິນຫລາຍ ແຕ່ກໍເປັນຄອບຄົວທີ່ມີຄວາມສຸກ .

ມື້ວານນີ້ຂ້ອຍໄປຊື້ເຄື່ອງຢູ່ທີ່ຕະຫລາດເຊົ້າ . ຊື້ເກີບມາ ຄູ່ນິ່ງ,
ຫືບສອງໝ່ວຍ,   ປຶ້ມສາມຫົວ, ປາກກາສີ່ກ້ານ, ແລະສໍຄໍາ
ຫ້າກ້ານ .

ໝູ່ສະໜິດຄົນນິ່ງຂອງຂ້ອຍຊື່ຄໍາແພງ . ລາວອາໄສຢູ່ເມືອງ
ຫລວງພະບາງ . ແຕ່ກ່ອນລາວຢູ່ເມືອງວຽງຈັນເຊິ່ງກຮຽວກັບ
ຂ້ອຍ . ພວກເຮົາເຄີຍໄປໂຮງຮຽນນໍາກັນ . ຂ້ອຍບໍ່ໄດ້ພົບກັບ
ລາວຫລາຍປີແລ້ວ, ແຕ່ພວກເຮົານໍາຕິດຕໍ່ກັນທາງຈົດໝາຍ
ຢູ່ສະເໝີ .

ນ້ອຍເປັນນັກສຶກສາຢູ່ທີ່ມະຫາວິທະຍາໄລ . ລາວກໍາລັງຮຽນວິຊາ
ພາສາອັງກິດເປັນວິຊາເອກ . ປີໜ້າລາວປາກຈະມາຮຽນ
ທີ່ອາເມລິກາ . ລາວມີອ້າຍເຮັດວຽກຢູ່ທີ່ແຂວງເຂ .

ເມືອງລາວມີອາຫານທີ່ແຊບຫລາຍປ່າງ. ຕົວຢ່າງເຂົ້ມ, ລາບ,
ຕໍາໝາກຫຸ່ງ, ແກງປາ, ໝົ້ງປາ. ອາຫານລາວອາດຜັກ
ແຕ່ສໍາລັບຂາວຕ່າງຂາດ, ແຕ່ຖ້າລິ້ງກັບລົດຂາດທີ່ຜັກແລ້ວ
ຈະຮູ້ວ່າອາຫານລາວແຊບຫລາຍ.

ຄົນລາວເປັນຂົນຂາດທີ່ມັກຄວາມມ່ວມຊົມ. ຄົນມັກມາໂຮມກັນ
ແລ້ວຈັດງານບຸນຕ່າງໆ. ມີການກິນອາຫານ, ຮ້ອງຣໍາ
ທໍາເພງ. ຄົນລາວຂີ່ວ່າຢູ່ບ່ອນໃດກໍຈະເອົາວັດທະມະທໍາ,
ປະເພນີຂອງຕົນໄປນໍາ.

ຕອນນີ້ຄອບຄົວຂອງຂ້ອຍອາໄສຢູ່ໃນອາເມລິກາ. ພວກເຮົາຍ້າຍ
ມາຢູ່ນີ້ໄດ້ຫົກປບຂາວປີແລ້ວ. ກ່ອນມາຢູ່ປະເທດນີ້, ພວກເຮົາຢູ່
ສູນສໍາລັບຜູ້ອົບພະຍົບທີ່ເມືອງໄທເປັນເວລາສາມປີ. ພວກເຮົາ
ມັກແລະຮັກອາເມລິກາຄືປະເທດຂອງຕົນເອງ.

Appendix I
Useful Words and Phrases

General Conversation

◆ Good morning. Good afternoon.   sa-bàai-dìi. ສະບາຍດີ.
  Good evening. Hello.

◆ How are you?   sa-bàai-dìi bɔɔ. ສະບາຍດີບໍ?

  Fine.   sa-bàai-dìi. ສະບາຍດີ.

  Not so good.   bɔɔ kɔi sa-bàai. ບໍ່ຄ່ອຍສະບາຍ.

  See you tomorrow.   mɯ̄ɯ ɯ̄ɯn pɔ̂ɔ gàn mai.
                                    ມື້ອື່ນພໍ້ກັນໃໝ່.

  See you later.   lɛ̂ɛo pɔ̂ɔ gàn mai. ແລ້ວພໍ້ກັນໃໝ່.

  Take care.   hak-sǎa dtùa-eeng dɛɛ dɔ̂ə.
                                    ຮັກສາຕົວເອງແດ່ເດີ.

◆ Thank you.   kɔ̀ɔp-jài. ຂອບໃຈ.

◆ Never mind./ You're welcome.   bɔɔ bpèn ñǎng. ບໍ່ເປັນຫຍັງ.

  Excuse me./ I'm sorry.   kɔ̌ɔ-tôot. ຂໍໂທດ.

  Nice to meet you.   ñín-dìi tii dâi pop jâo.
                                    ຍິນດີທີ່ໄດ້ພົບເຈົ້າ.

  How have you been doing?   jâo sa-bàai dìi yuu bɔɔ.
                                    ເຈົ້າສະບາຍດີຢູ່ບໍ?

  Long time no see.   bɔɔ dâi pop gàn dòn lɛ̂ɛo dée.
                                    ບໍ່ໄດ້ພົບກັນດົນແລ້ວເດ.

  This.   àn-nîi. ອັນນີ້.

  What's this?   àn-nii mɛɛn ñǎng.
                                    ອັນນີ້ແມ່ນຫຍັງ?

  That.   àn-nân. ອັນນັ້ນ.

◆ What's that?   àn-nân mɛɛn ñǎng.
                                    ອັນນັ້ນແມ່ນຫຍັງ?

◆ Here.   yuu nîi. ຢູ່ນີ້/ຢູ່ນີ້.

◆ There.   yuu nân. ຢູ່ນັ້ນ.

What?	ñǎng. ຫຍັງ?
Who?	pǎi. ໃຜ?
Whose?	kɔ̌ɔng-pǎi. ຂອງໃຜ?
Where?	yuu-sǎi. ຢູ່ໃສ?
When?	mɯa-dǎi. ເມື່ອໃດ?
Why?	bpèn-ñǎng. ເປັນຫຍັງ?
How?	yaang-dǎi./jang-dǎi. ຢ່າງໃດ?/ຈັ່ງໃດ?
How much?	tao-dǎi. ເທົ່າໃດ?
How much is this?	àn nîi láa-káa tao-dǎi. ອັນນີ້ລາຄາເທົ່າໃດ?
Hello (on the phone).	aa-lǒo. ອາໂຫຼ.
I'd like to speak (on the phone) with ____.	kɔ̀i kɔ̌ɔ wâo gǎp ____ dɛɛ. ຂ້ອຍຂໍເວົ້າກັບ ____ ແດ່.
Really?	mɛɛn tɛ̂ɛ bɔɔ. ແມ່ນແທ້ບໍ່?
Yes.	mɛɛn. ແມ່ນ.
No.	bɔɔ mɛɛn. ບໍ່ແມ່ນ.
If.	tàa. ຖ້າ.
Not yet.	ñáng tɯa. ຍັງເທື່ອ
Already.	lɛ̂ɛo. ແລ້ວ.
But.	dtɛɛ. ແຕ່.
Because.	pɔ-waa./ñɔ́ɔn-waa. ເພາະວ່າ/ຍ້ອນວ່າ.
Don't.	yaa. ຢ່າ.
Don't do it.	yaa het. ຢ່າເຮັດ.
O.K.	òo-kée./ɔ̀ɔ. ໂອເຄ/ເອີ.
So-so	jang sân là. ຈັ່ງຊັ້ນລະ.
Maybe	bàang-tîi. ບາງທີ.
Please	ga-lu-náa. ກະລຸນາ.

Where are you going?	jâo si bpài săi. ເຈົ້າຊິໄປໃສ?
Where have you been?	jâo bpài săi máa. ເຈົ້າໄປໃສມາ?
Have you eaten?	gìn kào lêεo bɔɔ. ກິນເຂົ້າແລ້ວບໍ?
◆ How's business?	tu-la-gĭt bpèn jang dăi.
	ທຸລະກິດເປັນຈັ່ງໃດ
What's your name?	jâo sɯɯ ñăng. ເຈົ້າຊື່ຫຍັງ?
My name is _____.	kɔ̀i sɯɯ _____..
	ຂ້ອຍຊື່ _____.
What kind of work do you do?	jâo het wĭak ñăng. ເຈົ້າເຮັດວຽກຫຍັງ?
I'm _____.	kɔ̀i bpèn _____.
	ຂ້ອຍເປັນ _____.
❏ A doctor	taan-mɔ̆ɔ ທ່ານໝໍ
❏ An engineer	wit-sa-wa-gɔ̀ɔn ວິສະວະກອນ
❏ A student	nak-hían ນັກຮຽນ
❏ A professor	sàat-sa-dàa-jàan ສາດສະດາຈານ
❏ A tourist	nak-tɔ̂ng-tiao ນັກທ່ອງທ່ຽວ
❏ A business person	nak-tu-la-gĭt ນັກທຸລະກິດ
Where are you from?	jâo máa jàak săi.
	ເຈົ້າມາຈາກໃສ?
◆ What country are you from?	jâo máa jàak bpa-têet dăi.
	ເຈົ້າມາຈາກປະເທດໃດ?
◆ I'm from _____.	kɔ̀i máa jàak _____.
	ຂ້ອຍມາຈາກ _____.
❏ America	àa-mée-li-gàa ອາເມລິກາ
❏ Japan	ñíi-bpun ຍີ່ປຸ່ນ
❏ England	àng-gĭt ອັງກິດ
❏ Germany	yɔ́əi-la-mán ເຍຍລະມັນ
❏ Australia	ot-sa-dtràa-líi ອົດສະຕຣາລີ

◆ Do you like Laos?   jâo mak mɨ́ang láao bɔɔ.
                                       ເຈົ້າມັກເມືອງລາວບໍ່?

Yes, very much.   mak lǎai. ມັກຫຼາຍ.

Do you like Lao food?   jâo mak àa-hǎan láao bɔɔ.
                                       ເຈົ້າມັກອາຫານລາວບໍ່?

Yes, I think it's very good.   mak kɔ̀i kit waa sɛ̂ɛp lǎai.
                                       ມັກ, ຂ້ອຍຄິດວ່າແຊບຫຼາຍ.

I think it's too spicy for me.   kɔ̀i kit waa mán pĕt gɔ̀ɔn
                                           bpài sǎm lǎp kɔ̀i.
                                       ຂ້ອຍຄິດວ່າມັນເຜັດເກີນໄປສຳລັບຂ້ອຍ.

What do you think about   jâo kit waa mɨ́ang láao
    Laos?   bpèn jang dǎi.
                                       ເຈົ້າຄິດວ່າເມືອງລາວເປັນຈັ່ງໃດ?

I think it's very beautiful.   kɔ̀i kit waa ngáam laai.
                                       ຂ້ອຍຄິດວ່າງາມຫຼາຍ.

I think it's a hard place   kɔ̀i kit waa yuu ñâak.
    to live in.   ຂ້ອຍຄິດວ່າມັນຢູ່ຍາກ.

I think it's very hot.   kɔ̀i kit waa hɔ̂ɔn lǎai.
                                       ຂ້ອຍຄິດວ່າຮ້ອນຫຼາຍ.

I like Vientiane.   kɔ̀i mak wíang-jàn.
                                       ຂ້ອຍມັກວຽງຈັນ.

◆ I don't like Vientiane.   kɔ̀i bɔɔ mak wíang-jàn.
                                       ຂ້ອຍບໍ່ມັກວຽງຈັນ.

Can you speak Lao?   jâo wâo láao dâi bɔɔ.
                                       ເຈົ້າເວົ້າລາວໄດ້ບໍ່?

Can you speak Thai?   jâo wâo tái dâi bɔɔ.
                                       ເຈົ້າເວົ້າໄທໄດ້ບໍ່?

Can you speak English?   jâo wâo páa-sǎa àng-gĭt
                                           dâi bɔɔ. ເຈົ້າເວົ້າພາສາອັງກິດໄດ້ບໍ່?

◆ (Please) speak more slowly.   (ga-lu-náa) wâo sâa-sâa dεε.
ꪁꪲ. (ꪀꪱꪶꪕꪱ) ꪒ꫁ꪱꪉꫛꪉꪵꪖꪈ.

◆ A little bit.   jǎk nɔi. ꪈꪰꪀꪘꪐꪮ꫁ꪥ.

◆ I'm studying Lao.   kɔi gàm-làng hían páa-sǎa láao.
ꪁꪮ꫁ꪥꪀꪾꪚ꫁ꪉꪽꪼꪬ꫁ꪅꪙꪽꪮꪱꪼꪳꪥꪚ꫁ꪜꪱ꫁ꪉꪺꪱꪼ꫁ꪔ꫁ꪱꪺ.

◆ I'm studying Lao from   kɔi gàm-làng hían páa-sǎa.
   this book.   láao jàak bpûm hǔa nîi.
ꪁꪮ꫁ꪥꪀꪾꪚ꫁ꪉꪽꪼꪬ꫁ꪮꪱꪼꪳꪥꪚ꫁ꪜꪱ꫁ꪉꪺꪱꪼ꫁ꪔ꫁ꪺꪉꪀꪀꪺꪱꪜꪲ꫁ꪣꪬꪲꪺꪚꪲ꫁.

◆ Where did you learn English?   jâo hían páa-sǎa àng-gǐt
       yuu-sai.
ꪵꪊ꫁ꪱꪼ꫁ꪬꪽꪜꪱ꫁ꪉꪺꪱꪮꪰꪉꪀꪲꪒꪚꪴ꫁ꪼ꫁ꪹ?

◆ How do you say this in Lao?   kám nîi páa-sǎa láao waa
       jang-dǎi.
ꪁꪾꪚꪲ꫁ꪜꪱ꫁ꪉꪺꪱꪼ꫁ꪺ꫁ꪱꪊꪰ꫁ꪉꪼꪒ?

◆ How do you read this in Lao?   kám nîi páa-sǎa láao waa
       jang dǎi.
ꪁꪾꪚꪲ꫁ꪜꪱ꫁ꪉꪺꪱꪼ꫁ꪮꪱꪻꪺ꫁ꪱꪊꪰ꫁ꪉꪼꪒ?

◆ What does this mean?   àn nîi mǎai-kwáam waa
       jang dǎi.
ꪮꪽꪚꪲ꫁ꪫꪱꪥꪁꪺꪱꪣꪺ꫁ꪱꪊꪰ꫁ꪉꪼꪒ?

◆ What does ____ mean?   ____ mǎai-kwáam waa
       jang dǎi.
____ ꪫꪱꪥꪁꪺꪱꪣꪺ꫁ꪱꪊꪰ꫁ꪉꪼꪒ?

◆ How old are you?   jâo àa-ñu tao dǎi.
ꪹꪊ꫁ꪱꪮꪱꪥꪴꪹꪕꪱ꫁ꪻꪒ?

◆ I'm ____ years old.   kɔi àa-ñu ____ bpìi.
ꪁꪮ꫁ꪥꪮꪱꪥꪴ____ ꪜꪲ.

◆ Where do you live?   hûan jâo yuu sǎi.
   (Where is your house?)   ꪹꪣꪮꪙꪹꪊ꫁ꪱꪥꪴꪻ?

I live in _____.   kɔ̀i yuu tii _____.

ຂ້ອຍຢູ່ທີ່ _____.

My house is_____.   hǔan kɔ̀i yuu _____.

ເຮືອນຂ້ອຍຢູ່ _____.

My house is not far from here.   hǔan kɔ̀i yuu bɔɔ gài jàak nîi.

ເຮືອນຂ້ອຍຢູ່ບໍ່ໄກຈາກນີ້.

Do you have brothers or   jâo mǐi pii nɔ̂ɔng bɔɔ.

sisters?   ເຈົ້າມີພີ່ນ້ອງບໍ່?

How many brothers and   jâo mǐi pii nɔ̂ɔng jǎk kón.

sisters do you have?   ເຈົ້າມີພີ່ນ້ອງຈັກຄົນ?

Are you married?   jâo dtɛng-ngáan lɛ̂ɛo bɔɔ.

ເຈົ້າແຕ່ງງານແລ້ວບໍ່?

I'm married.   kɔ̀i dtɛng-ngáan lɛ̂ɛo.

ຂ້ອຍແຕ່ງງານແລ້ວ.

I'm not married.   kɔ̀i ñáng bɔɔ tán

dtɛng-ngáan tɯa.

ຂ້ອຍຍັງບໍ່ທັນແຕ່ງງານເທື່ອ.

I'm divorced.   kɔ̀i bpèn (pɔɔ/mɛɛ) hâang.

ຂ້ອຍເປັນ (ພໍ່/ແມ່) ຮ້າງ.

I'm single.   kɔ̀i bpèn sòot.

ຂ້ອຍເປັນໂສດ.

How's your family?   kɔ̂ɔp-kúa jâo bpèn jang-dai.

ຄອບຄົວເຈົ້າເປັນຈັ່ງໃດ?

◆ How's the weather?   àa-gàat bpèn jang-dǎi.

ອາກາດເປັນຈັ່ງໃດ?

It's hot.   hɔ̂ɔn. ຮ້ອນ.

It's cold.   nǎao. ໜາວ.

◆ Are you free tonight?   mɯ̂ɯ lɛ́ɛng nîi jâo waang bɔɔ.

ມື້ແລງນີ້ເຈົ້າຫວ່າງບໍ່?

Can I see you tomorrow? — kòi pop jâo mûu uun dâi bɔɔ.

ຂ້ອຍພົບເຈົ້າມື້ອື່ນໄດ້ບໍ່?

Are you free next Friday night? — kûun wán sǔk nàa jâo waang bɔɔ.

ຄືນວັນສຸກໜ້າເຈົ້າຫວ່າງບໍ່?

Can you teach me Lao? — jâo sɔ̌ɔn páa-sǎa láao hài kòi dâi bɔɔ.

ເຈົ້າສອນພາສາລາວໃຫ້ຂ້ອຍໄດ້ບໍ່?

I like _____. — kòi mak _____.

ຂ້ອຍມັກ _____.

I don't like _____. — kòi bɔɔ mak _____.

ຂ້ອຍບໍ່ມັກ _____.

I like Lao people. — kòi mak kón láao.

ຂ້ອຍມັກຄົນລາວ.

I don't like lazy people. — kòi bɔɔ mak kón kîi-kâan.

ຂ້ອຍບໍ່ມັກຄົນຂີ້ຄ້ານ.

You are kind. — jâo jài-dìi. ເຈົ້າໃຈດີ.

Where are you staying? — jâo pak yuu sǎi. ເຈົ້າພັກຢູ່ໃສ?

I'm staying at the Grand Hotel. — kòi pak yuu hóong-héεm grèen.

ຂ້ອຍພັກຢູ່ໂຮງແຮມແກຣນ.

I enjoy talking with you. — kòi mak lóm gǎp jâo.

ຂ້ອຍມັກລົມກັບເຈົ້າ.

Here is my address. — nîi mεεn tii-yuu kɔ̌ɔng kòi.

ນີ້ແມ່ນທີ່ຢູ່ຂອງຂ້ອຍ.

Here is my phone number. — nîi mεεn lêek tóo kɔ̌ɔng kòi.

ນີ້ແມ່ນເລກໂທຂອງຂ້ອຍ.

◆ Can I have your address? — kòi kɔ̌ɔ tii-yuu jâo dâi bɔɔ.

ຂ້ອຍຂໍທີ່ຢູ່ເຈົ້າໄດ້ບໍ່?

Can I have your phone number? kɔ̀i kɔ̌ɔ nâam-bəə-tóo-la-
                                                   sǎp jâo dâi bɔɔ.

ຂ້ອຍຂໍບ້າເບິໂທລະສັບເຈົ້າໄດ້ບໍ?

Give me a call.   tóo hǎa kɔ̀i dɛɛ dəə.

ໂທຫາຂ້ອຍແດ່ເດີ.

I will give you a call.   kɔ̀i ja tóo hǎa jâo.

ຂ້ອຍຈະໂທຫາເຈົ້າ.

Can I call you?   kɔ̀i tóo hǎa jâo dâi bɔɔ.

ຂ້ອຍໂທຫາເຈົ້າໄດ້ບໍ?

I want to see you again.   kɔ̀i yàak pop jâo ìik.

ຂ້ອຍຢາກພົບເຈົ້າອີກ.

I like you.   kɔ̀i mak jâo. ຂ້ອຍມັກເຈົ້າ.

I'm leaving tomorrow.   kɔ̀i ja bpài mʉ̀ʉ-ʉʉn.

ຂ້ອຍຈະໄປມື້ອື່ນ.

◆ I'm going back to my   àa-tit nàa kɔ̀i ja gǎp kʉ̀ʉn
   country next week.   bpa-têet kɔ̌ɔng kɔ̀i.

ອາທິດໜ້າ ຂ້ອຍຈະກັບຄືນປະເທດຂອງຂ້ອຍ.

I will come to Laos again.   kɔ̀i ja máa mʉ̀ang láao ìik.

ຂ້ອຍຈະມາເມືອງລາວອີກ.

I will think about you.   kɔ̀i ja kit hɔ̌ɔt jâo.

ຂ້ອຍຈະຄຶດຮອດເຈົ້າ.

◆ I will miss you.   kɔ̀i kóng ja kit hɔ̌ɔt jâo.

ຂ້ອຍຄົງຈະຄຶດຮອດເຈົ້າ.

◆ I will keep in touch.   kɔ̀i ja dtǐt-dtɔɔ hǎa jâo
                                                   lʉ̂ai- lʉ̂ai.

ຂ້ອຍຈະຕິດຕໍ່ຫາເຈົ້າເລື້ອຍໆ.

◆ Don't forget me.   yaa lʉ́ʉm kɔ̀i dəə. ຢ່າລືມຂ້ອຍເດີ.

In a Restaurant

◆ I want to order _____.

kòi yàak sang _____.
ຂ້ອຍປາກສັ່ງ _____.

◆ What would you like to eat?

jâo yàak gìn ñǎng.
ເຈົ້າຢາກກິນຫຍັງ?

◆ What would you like to drink?

jâo yàak dɯɯm ñǎng.
ເຈົ້າຢາກດື່ມຫຍັງ?

◆ I'd like a glass of water.

kòi yàak dɯɯm nâam jɔɔk
nɯng. ຂ້ອຍປາກດື່ມນ້ຳຈອກນຶ່ງ.

◆ I'd like one serving of
   fried rice.

kòi yàak dâi kào pǎt jàan
nɯng. ຂ້ອຍປາກໄດ້ເຂົ້າຜັດຈານນຶ່ງ.

◆ I'd like some ice.

kòi yàak dâi nâam gɔ̂ɔn.
ຂ້ອຍປາກໄດ້ນ້ຳກ້ອນ.

◆ Is it spicy?

mán pět bɔɔ. ມັນເຜັດບໍ່?

◆ This is too spicy.

àn-nîi pět pôot. ອັນນີ້ເຜັດໂພດ.

◆ This is not spicy.

àn-nîi bɔɔ pět. ອັນນີ້ບໍ່ເຜັດ.

◆ Is it delicious?

àn-nîi sɛ̂ɛp bɔɔ. ອັນນີ້ແຊບບໍ່?

◆ It's delicious.

sɛ̂ɛp. ແຊບ.

◆ It's not delicious.

bɔɔ sɛ̂ɛp. ບໍ່ແຊບ.

◆ The food is very delicious.

àa-hǎan sɛ̂ɛp lǎai.
ອາຫານແຊບຫລາຍ.

◆ I like Lao food.

kòi mak àa-hǎan láao.
ຂ້ອຍມັກອາຫານລາວ.

◆ I want some dessert.

kòi yàak gìn kɔ̌ɔng wǎan.
ຂ້ອຍປາກກິນຂອງຫວານ.

◆ I'm already full.

kòi im lɛ̂ɛo. ຂ້ອຍອີ່ມແລ້ວ.

◆ That's enough.

pɔ̂ɔ lɛ̂ɛo. ພໍແລ້ວ.

◆ I'm drunk.

kòi máo lào. ຂ້ອຍເມົາເຫລົ້າ.

◆ Please give me the bill.   kit ngán dεε. ຄິດເງິນແດ່?

◆ The food is not expensive.   àa-hǎan bɔɔ péeng.
                                       ອາຫານບໍ່ແພງ.

◆ Do I need to leave a tip?   kòi dtông hài tip bɔɔ.
                                       ຂ້ອຍຕ້ອງໃຫ້ທິບບໍ່?

◆ Menu   mée-núu/láai-gàan-àa-hǎan
                                       ເມນູ/ລາຍການອາຫານ

❏ bake/baked   ǒp ອົບ

❏ beer   bìa ເບຍ

❏ beef   sìin-ngúa ຊີ້ນງົວ

❏ boil/boiled   dtôm ຕົ້ມ

❏ chicken   gai ໄກ່

❏ coffee   gàa-fée ກາເຟ

❏ crab   ga-bpùu ກະປູ

❏ curry   gὲεng-ga-lii ແກງກະຫລີ່

❏ dessert   kɔ̌ɔng wǎan ຂອງຫວານ

❏ delicious   sὲεp ແຊບ

❏ duck   bpĕt ເປັດ

❏ eat   gìn ກິນ

❏ egg   kai ໄຂ່

❏ fish   bpàa ປາ

❏ food   àa-hǎan ອາຫານ

❏ fry/fried   jʉʉn ຈືນ

❏ fruit   màak-mâi ຫມາກໄມ້

❏ grill/grilled   bpîng ປີ້ງ

❏ ice   nâam-gɔ̂ɔn ນ້ຳກ້ອນ

❏ noodles   fǒǝ ເຝີ

❏ orange juice   nâam-màak-gîang ນ້ຳຫມາກກ້ຽງ

❏ pork   sìin-mǔu ຊີ້ນຫມູ

☐ porridge   kào-bpìak เຂົ້າປຽກ

☐ rice   kào เຂົ້າ

☐ seafood   àa-hăan-ta-lée ອາຫານທະເລ

☐ shrimp   gûng ກຸ້ງ

☐ snack   àa-hăan-waang ອາຫານຫວ່າງ

☐ soup   gὲεng ແກງ

☐ squid   bpàa-mŭk ປາໝຶກ

☐ sticky rice   kào-nĭao เຂົ້າໜຽວ

☐ tea   sáa ຊາ

☐ Lao food   àa-hăan-láao ອາຫານລາວ

☐ turkey   gai-ngúang ໄກ່ງວງ

☐ vegetable   păk ຜັກ

☐ vegetarian   àa-hăan-păk/jὲe ອາຫານຜັກ/ເຈ

☐ whisky   lào ເຫຼົ້າ

☐ wine   lào-wὲεng ເຫຼົ້າແວງ

Expressing Needs and Feelings

I'm hungry.	kɔ̀i hǐu kào./kɔ̀i yàak kào.
	ຂ້ອຍຫິວເຂົ້າ./ຂ້ອຍປາກເຂົ້າ.
I'm thirsty.	kɔ̀i yàak nâam. ຂ້ອຍປາກນ້ຳ.
I'm tired.	kɔ̀i mɯai. ຂ້ອຍເມື່ອຍ.
I'm exhausted.	kɔ̀i hûu-sɯ̌k mót-hέεng.
	ຂ້ອຍຮູ້ສຶກໝົດແຮງ.
I'm sleepy.	kɔ̀i ngǎo-nɔ́ɔn. ຂ້ອຍເຫງົານອນ.
I'm excited.	kɔ̀i dtɯɯn-dtên. ຂ້ອຍຕື່ນເຕັ້ນ.
I'm hot.	kɔ̀i hɔ̂ɔn. ຂ້ອຍຮ້ອນ.
I'm cold.	kɔ̀i nǎao. ຂ້ອຍໜາວ.
◆ I feel sick.	kɔ̀i bɔɔ sa-bàai. ຂ້ອຍບໍ່ສະບາຍ.
I have a headache.	kɔ̀i jĕp hǔa. ຂ້ອຍເຈັບຫົວ.
I have a stomach ache.	kɔ̀i jĕp tɔ̂ɔng. ຂ້ອຍເຈັບທ້ອງ.
I have diarrhea.	kɔ̀i mǐi àa-gàan-sɯ̌-tɔ̂ɔng.
	ຂ້ອຍມີອາການສຸທ້ອງ.
◆ I have jet-lag.	kɔ̀i bpǎp wée-láa bɔɔ tán.
	ຂ້ອຍປັບເວລາບໍ່ທັນ.
◆ I need some medicine.	kɔ̀i yàak dâi yàa. ຂ້ອຍປາກໄດ້ຢາ.
I need some rest.	kɔ̀i yàak pak jǎk nɔi.
	ຂ້ອຍປາກພັກຈັກໜ່ອຍ.
◆ I want to see a doctor.	kɔ̀i yàak bpài hǎa taan mɔ̌ɔ.
	ຂ້ອຍປາກໄປຫາທ່ານໝໍ.
I need help.	kɔ̀i dtɔ̂ng gàan kwáam sɔɔi-lǔa.
	ຂ້ອຍຕ້ອງການການຊ່ອຍເຫລືອ.
Come here.	máa-nîi. ມານີ້.
◆ Help!	sɔɔi dɛɛ. ຊ່ອຍແດ່!
◆ Watch out!	la-wáng. ລະວັງ!

I want to drink some water.   kɔ̀i yàak dʉʉm nâam.

ອ້ອຍປາກດື່ມນ້ຳ.

I want to have some   kɔ̀i yàak gìn bìa.

beer.   ອ້ອຍປາກກິນເບຍ.

I want to have a cup   kɔ̀i yàak gìn gàa-fée jɔɔk nʉng.

of coffee.   ອ້ອຍປາກກິນກາເຟຈອກໜຶ່ງ.

I want to buy some   kɔ̀i yàak sʉ̂ʉ yàa-sùup.

cigarettes.   ອ້ອຍປາກຊື້ຢາສູບ.

I want to buy some   kɔ̀i yàak sʉ̂ʉ yàa.

medicine.   ອ້ອຍປາກຊື້ຢາ.

I want to use the restroom.   kɔ̀i yàak kào hɔ̀ng nâam.

ອ້ອຍປາກເຂົ້າຫ້ອງນ້ຳ.

Where is the restroom?   hɔ̀ng-nâam yuu sǎi. ຫ້ອງນ້ຳຢູ່ໃສ?

It's too loud.   sǐang dàng pôot. ສຽງດັງໂພດ.

Can you turn down   jâo pɔn ɛ̀ɛ lóng dɛɛ

the air-conditioner?   dâi bɔɔ. ເຈົ້າຜ່ອນແອລົງແດໄດ້ບໍ່?

Can you turn up   jâo bpə̀ət ɛ̀ɛ kʉ̀n dtʉʉm dɛɛ

the air-conditioner?   dâi bɔɔ. ເຈົ້າເປີດແອຂຶ້ນຕື່ມແດໄດ້ບໍ່?

Turn on the fan.   bpə̀ət pat-lóm. ເປີດພັດລົມ.

It's very hot and stuffy   yuu nîi hɔ̂ɔn lɛ ǒp-âo

in here.   lǎai. ຢູ່ນີ້ຮ້ອນແລະອົບເອົ້າຫລາຍ.

Can I use the telephone?   kɔ̀i kɔ̌ɔ sâi tóo-la-sǎp dɛɛ

dâi bɔɔ. ອ້ອຍຂໍໃຊ້ໂທລະສັບແດໄດ້ບໍ່?

Can I have more water?   kɔ̀i kɔ̌ɔ nâam dtʉʉm

ìik dɛɛ. ອ້ອຍຂໍນ້ຳດື່ມອີກແດ່.

I'm lost.   kɔ̀i lǒng táang. ອ້ອຍຫລົງທາງ.

How do I go to ____?   kɔ̀i ja bpài ____ dâi jang

dǎi. ອ້ອຍຈະໄປ _____ ໄດ້ຈັ່ງໃດ?

I need more money.   kɔ̀i dtôŋ gàan ŋən dtɯɯm ìik.
ຂ້ອຍຕ້ອງການເງິນເພີ່ມອີກ.

I need to go to the bank.   kɔ̀i dtôŋ bpài ta-náa-káan.
ຂ້ອຍຕ້ອງໄປທະນາຄານ.

I need to exchange money.   kɔ̀i yàak bpian ŋən.
ຂ້ອຍປາກປ່ຽນເງິນ.

I need to call a taxi.   kɔ̀i dtôŋ tóo ɔ̂ən lot dtak-sîi.
ຂ້ອຍຕ້ອງໃຫເອີ້ນລົດຕັກຊີ່.

◆ I want to go home.   kɔ̀i yàak bpài hɯan.
ຂ້ອຍປາກໄປເຮືອນ.

I want to _____ (verb).   kɔ̀i dtôŋ gàan_____.
ຂ້ອຍຕ້ອງການ _____.

                                            kɔ̀i yàak ___. ຂ້ອຍປາກ ___.

I want _____ (noun).   kɔ̀i dtôŋ-gàan _____. /
                                            • kɔ̀i yàak dâi _____.
ຂ້ອຍຕ້ອງການ _____. /
ຂ້ອຍປາກໄດ້ _____.

Give me _____.   ào _____ hài kɔ̀i dɛɛ.
ເອົາ _____ ໃຫ້ຂ້ອຍແດ່.

Give me a pen.   kɔ̌ɔ bpàak-gàa dɛɛ. ຂໍປາກກາແດ່.

I have a question.   kɔ̀i mǐi kám-tǎam. ຂ້ອຍມີຄຳຖາມ.

I have to leave.   kɔ̀i dtôŋ bpài lɛ̂ɛo là.
ຂ້ອຍຕ້ອງໄປແລ້ວລະ.

I have to go back to   kɔ̀i dtôŋ găp hóoŋ-héɛm
   my hotel.   lɛ̂ɛo là. ຂ້ອຍຕ້ອງກັບໂຮງແຮມແລ້ວລະ.

I'm leaving tomorrow.   kɔ̀i ja mɯ̂a mɯ̂ɯ-ɯɯn.
ຂ້ອຍຈະເມືອມື້ອື່ນ.

I'm going back to   kɔ̀i ja găp kɯɯn bpa-têet
   my country.   kɔ̌ɔŋ kɔ̀i.
ຂ້ອຍຈະກັບຄືນປະເທດຂອງຂ້ອຍ.

I understand.	kɔ̀i kào jài. ຂ້ອຍເຂົ້າໃຈ.
I don't understand.	kɔ̀i bɔɔ kào jài. ຂ້ອຍບໍ່ເຂົ້າໃຈ.
I don't know.	kɔ̀i bɔɔ hûu. ຂ້ອຍບໍ່ຮູ້.
I think so, too.	kɔ̀i kit jang-sân kúu-gàn. ຂ້ອຍຄິດຈັ່ງຊັ້ນຄືກັນ.
I don't think so.	kɔ̀i bɔɔ kit nέεo nân. ຂ້ອຍບໍ່ຄິດແນວນັ້ນ.
I believe you.	kɔ̀i sʉa jâo. ຂ້ອຍເຊື່ອເຈົ້າ.
I don't believe you.	kɔ̀i bɔɔ sʉa jâo. ຂ້ອຍບໍ່ເຊື່ອເຈົ້າ.
I'm sure.	kɔ̀i nεε-jài. ຂ້ອຍແນ່ໃຈ.
I'm not sure.	kɔ̀i bɔɔ nεε-jài. ຂ້ອຍບໍ່ແນ່ໃຈ.
I'm joking.	kɔ̀i wâo lìn. ຂ້ອຍເວົ້າຫລິ້ນ.
I like it.	kɔ̀i mak. ຂ້ອຍມັກ.
I like it very much.	kɔ̀i mak lǎai. ຂ້ອຍມັກຫລາຍ.
I don't like it.	kɔ̀i bɔɔ mak. ຂ້ອຍບໍ່ມັກ.
I forgot.	kɔ̀i lʉʉm. ຂ້ອຍລືມ.
I remember.	kɔ̀i jʉʉ dâi. ຂ້ອຍຈື່ໄດ້.
I don't remember.	kɔ̀i jʉʉ bɔɔ dâi. ຂ້ອຍຈື່ບໍ່ໄດ້.
Is that right?	tʉ̀ʉk bɔɔ. ຖືກບໍ່?
No problem.	bɔɔ mîi bàn-hǎa. ບໍ່ມີບັນຫາ.
That's interesting.	nàa-sǒn-jài. ໜ້າສົນໃຈ.
Let's go.	bpài gàn tɔ. ໄປກັນເຖາະ.
Are you ready/finished?	jâo lɛ̂εo lɛ̂εo bɔɔ. ເຈົ້າແລ້ວແລ້ວບໍ່?
May I smoke?	kɔ̀i kɔ̌ɔ sùup yàa dâi bɔɔ. ຂ້ອຍຂໍສູບຢາໄດ້ບໍ່?
No smoking.	hàam sùup yàa. ຫ້າມສູບຢາ.
I'm ready.	kɔ̀i pɔ̂ɔm lɛ̂εo. ຂ້ອຍພ້ອມແລ້ວ.

I'm not ready. kòi ñáng bɔɔ pɔɔm.
ຂ້ອຍຍັງບໍ່ພ້ອມ.

I'm busy. kòi káa wìak. ຂ້ອຍຄາວຽກ.

I'm happy. kòi mîi kwáam sǔk.
ຂ້ອຍມີຄວາມສຸກ.

I'm enjoying myself. kòi muan. ຂ້ອຍມ່ວນ.

I'm sad. kòi sào-jài. ຂ້ອຍເສົ້າໃຈ.

I'm fine. kòi sa-bàai-dìi. ຂ້ອຍສະບາຍດີ.

I'm angry. kòi jài hâai. ຂ້ອຍໃຈຮ້າຍ.

I'm mad at you. kòi kìat hài jâo. ຂ້ອຍຄຽດໃຫ້ເຈົ້າ.

I'm lonely. kòi ngǎo. ຂ້ອຍເຫງົ່າ.

I'm surprised. kòi bpa-làat-jài. ຂ້ອຍປະຫລາດໃຈ.

I'm disappointed. kòi pǐt-wǎng. ຂ້ອຍຜິດຫວັງ.

I'm worried. kòi gàng-wón-jài. ຂ້ອຍກັງວົນໃຈ.

I'm worried about you. kòi bpèn-huang jâo.
ຂ້ອຍເປັນຫ່ວງເຈົ້າ.

I'm confused. kòi sǎp-sǒn. ຂ້ອຍສັບສົນ.

I'm hurt (emotionally). kòi jěp-jài. ຂ້ອຍເຈັບໃຈ.

It's embarrassing. mán bpèn-dtɛɛ-nàa-àai.
ມັນເປັນແຕ່ໜ້າອາຍ.

I'm desperate. kòi mǒt-wǎng. ຂ້ອຍໝົດຫວັງ.

I envy you. kòi ǐt-sǎa-jâo. ຂ້ອຍອິດສາເຈົ້າ.

I have a broken heart. kòi ǒk-hǎk. ຂ້ອຍອົກຫັກ.

I don't want to promise. kòi bɔɔ yàak hài sǎn-ñáa.
ຂ້ອຍບໍ່ຢາກໃຫ້ສັນຍາ.

It's boring. bpèn-dtàa-bɨa. ເປັນຕາເບື່ອ.

I am homesick. kòi kit-hɔ̂ɔt bâan.
ຂ້ອຍຄິດຮອດບ້ານ.

I made a mistake. kòi het pǐt-pâat bpài.
ຂ້ອຍເຮັດຜິດພາດໄປ.

◆   I agree with you.   kòi hĕn pɔ̂ɔm nám jâo.
                                     ຂ້ອຍເຫັນພ້ອມນຳເຈົ້າ.

◆   I don't agree with you.   kòi bɔɔ hĕn pɔ̂ɔm nám jâo.
                                     ຂ້ອຍບໍ່ເຫັນພ້ອມນຳເຈົ້າ.

◆   Listen!   fáng./fáng nîi gɔɔn. ຟັງ!/ຟັງນີ້ກ່ອນ!

◆   Look!   bəng hàn./bəng mɛ̌ɛ./bəng dtĭi.
                                     ເບິ່ງຫັ້ນ!/ເບິ່ງແມ່!/ເບິ່ງຕີ!

◆   A little bit.   nɔ̀i nung. ໜ້ອຍນຶ່ງ.

◆   Very. A lot.   lăai. ຫລາຍ.

◆   Speak more slowly.   wâo sâa-sâa gwaa nîi.
                                     ເວົ້າຊ້າໆກວ່ານີ້.

◆   Speak up!   wâo dàng-dàng. ເວົ້າດັງໆ!

◆   Say it again.   wâo ìik tɨa. ເວົ້າອີກເທື່ອ.

                                     kɨɨn wâo ìik duu. ຄືນເວົ້າອີກດູ່.

◆   I can't hear.   kòi bɔɔ dâi ñín. ຂ້ອຍບໍ່ໄດ້ຍິນ.

◆   Be careful.   la-wáng. ລະວັງ.

◆   Wait a minute.   tàa bŭt-nung. ຖ້າບຶດນຶ່ງ.

◆   It's too loud.   sĭang-dàng pôot. ສຽງດັງໂພດ.

◆   Happy Birthday!   sŭk-săn wán gə̀ət.
                                     ສຸກສັນວັນເກີດ!

◆   Merry Christmas!   sŭk-săn wán kit-sa-mâat.
                                     ສຸກສັນວັນຄຣິສມາສ!

◆   Congratulations!   kɔ̌ɔ sa-dèɛng kwáam ñín
                                       dìi nám.
                                     ຂໍສະແດງຄວາມຍິນດີນຳ!

◆   I'm sorry to hear that.   kòi sĭa-jài dûai. ຂ້ອຍເສຍໃຈດ້ວຍ.

◆   I wish you happiness.   kɔ̌ɔ hài mĭi kwáam sŭk.
                                     ຂໍໃຫ້ມີຄວາມສຸກ.

◆ I wish you lots of happiness.   kɔ̌ɔ hài mɨ́i kwáam-sǔk
                                      lǎai-lǎai.

ຂໍໃຫ້ມີຄວາມສຸກຫລາຍໆ.

◆ I'm happy for you.   kɔ̀i dìi-jài nám.

ຂ້ອຍດີໃຈນຳ.

◆ I'm sorry for you.   kɔ̀i sǐa-jài nám.

ຂ້ອຍເສຍໃຈນຳ.

◆ Amen.   àa-méen/sǎa-tu.

ອາເມນ/ສາທຸ

◆ Wow!   ôo.

ໂອ້!

◆ Good luck.   sôok-dìi/kɔ̌ɔ hài sôok-dìi.

ໂຊກດີ./ຂໍໃຫ້ໂຊກດີ.

◆ I wish you good health.   kɔ̌ɔ hài yuu dii mɨ́i héng.

ຂໍໃຫ້ຢູ່ດີມີແຮງ.

Appendix II
Summary of the Lao Writing System

Lao Spelling Inconsistencies

You may encounter different ways of spelling a word in different dictionaries or by different people and wonder about the inconsistencies. Many Lao people left the country because of the political situation in the 1970's. They are used to the old writing system, which is more complicated (it is similar to written Thai) than the current system. Other Lao people may write words exactly the way they hear them, regardless of the official spelling. The Lao Ministry of Education has standardized the spelling and writing system but you will still see many variants.

Here are some examples of spelling variations that you may come across:

ເບຍ (beer) may be seen written as ເບຍ, ເບຍຣ, ເບັຍ, ເບັຍຣ.
ເລື່ອງ (story, matter) may be seen written as ເລື້ອງ, ເລື່ອງ.
ໄລຍະ (distance) may be seen written as ໄລຍະ, ລະຍະ.
ເພີ່ມ (add) may be seen written as ເພີ້ມ, ເພີ່ມ.
ກຶ່ນ (ground) may be seen written as ກຶ່ນ, ກຶ່ນ.
ໂລກ (world, disease) may be seen written as ໂລກ, ໂຣກ.
ຫລາຍ (many) may be seen written as ຫລາຍ, ຫຼາຍ.
ຮັບ (receive) may be seen written as ຮັບ, ຮັບ, ລັບ.
ໂຮງແຮມ (hotel) may be seen written as ໂຮງແຮມ, ໂຮງແຮມ.
ກຳນົດ (set, establish) may be seen written as ກຳນົດ, ກຳໜົດ.

The letter ຣ /r/ is not officially listed in the current Lao writing system. However, you will see it written sporadically. Lao people no longer pronounce the /r/, having replaced it entirely with the /l/ sound. Therefore, it was removed from the alphabet during the Ministry of Education's standardization of the writing system and replaced with ລ /l/ wherever it had occurred. Sometimes people still use the ຣ to transliterate foreign words into Lao. For example, ຝຣັ່ງ (foreigner or Caucasian) is often written with the ຣ, but is still pronounced with the /l/ sound.

26 Lao Consonants in Alphabetical Order

ກ°   ຂ•   ຄ△   ງ△

ຈ°   ສ•   ຊ△   ຍ△

ດ°   ຕ°   ຖ•   ທ△

ນ△   ບ°   ປ°   ຜ•

ຝ•   ພ△   ຟ△   ມ△

ຢ°   ລ△   ວ△   ຫ•

ອ°   ຣ△

s /r/ is not listed here. It is no longer officially in the Lao writing
system, but may still be seen written here and there (many times
with foreign words). When it occurs it is pronounced as /l/.

• 6 High consonants

◇ 8 Mid consonants

△ 12 Low consonants

Consonant	Consonant Name	Sound
ກ ໋	ກ ໄກ່ gɔ̀ɔ gai - chicken	/g/
ຂ ໋	ຂ ໄຂ່ kɔ̌ɔ kai - egg	/k/
ຄ ໋	ຄ ຄວາຍ kɔ́ɔ kwáai - buffalo	/k/
ງ ໋	ງ ງົວ ngɔ́ɔ ngúa - cow	/ng/
ຈ ໋	ຈ ຈອກ jɔ̀ɔ jɔ̀ɔk - cup, glass	/j/
ສ ໋	ສ ເສືອ sɔ̌ɔ sǔa - tiger	/s/
ຊ ໋	ຊ ຊ້າງ sɔ́ɔ sâang - elephant	/s/
ຍ ໋	ຍ ຍຸງ ñɔ́ɔ ñúng - mosquito	/ñ/, /ny/
ດ ໋	ດ ເດັກ dɔ̀ɔ děk - child	/d/
ຕ ໋	ຕ ຕາ dtɔ̀ɔ dtàa - eye	/dt/
ຖ ໋	ຖ ຖົງ tɔ̌ɔ tǒng - bag	/t/
ທ ໋	ທ ທຸງ tɔ́ɔ túng - flag	/t/
ນ ໋	ນ ນົກ nɔ́ɔ nok - bird	/n/
ບ ໋	ບ ແບບ bɔ̀ɔ bɛ̂ɛ - goat	/b/

ປ໌   ປ ປາ   bpɔɔ bpàa - fish   /bp/

ຜ໌   ຜ ເຜີ້ງ   pɔɔ pèng - bee   /p/

ຝ໌   ຝ ຝົນ   fɔɔ fŏn - rain   /f/

ພᐃ   ພ ພູ   pɔɔ púu - mountain   /p/

ຟᐃ   ຟ ໄຟ   fɔɔ faí - fire   /f/

ມᐃ   ມ ແມວ   mɔɔ méεo - cat   /m/

ຢ໌   ຢ ຢາ   yɔɔ yàa - medicine   /y/

ລᐃ   ລ ລີງ   lɔɔ líng - monkey   /l/

ວᐃ   ວ ວີ   wɔɔ wíi - fan   /w/

ຫ໌   ຫ ຫ່ານ   hɔɔ haan - goose   /h/

ອ໌   ອ ໂອ   ɔɔ òo - bowl   /ɔ/

ຮᐃ   ຮ ເຮືອນ hɔɔ húan - house   /h/

• 6 High consonants
◇ 8 Mid consonants
ᐃ 12 Low consonants

28 Lao Vowels in Alphabetical Order

ໍ

Lao Vowels Paired With Short and Long Counterparts

Short vowels are displayed in the left column and their counterparts (long vowels) are on the right.

Short Vowel		Long Vowel	
ເໂ	/ă/	ອາ	/àa/
◌	/ĭ/	◌	/ĭi/
◌	/ŭ/	◌	/ʉʉ/
◌	/ŭ/	◌	/ùu/

ເຊະ	/ĕe/	ເຊ	/ēe/
ແຊະ	/ɛ̆/	ແຊ	/ɛ̄ɛ/
ໂຊະ	/ŏ/	ໂຊ	/ōo/
ເຊາະ	/ɔ̆/	◌ໍ	/ɔ̄ɔ/
ເຊິ	/ə̆/	ເຊີ	/ə̄ə/
ເຊຍ	/ĭa/	ເຍ	/ia/
ເຊຶອ	/ŭa/	ເຊືອ	/ua/
◌ົວະ	/ŭa/	◌ົວ	/ua/

The following vowels may sound either short or long, but they are categorized as long vowels for tone rule purposes. Sometimes they are called "special vowels."

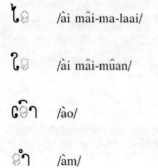

ໄຊ   /ài mâi-ma-laai/

ໃຊ   /ài mâi-mûan/

ເຊົາ   /ào/

◌ໍາ   /àm/

Lao Numbers

໐	ສູນ	sǔun	0
໑	ນຶ່ງ	nɯng	1
໒	ສອງ	sɔ̌ɔng	2
໓	ສາມ	sǎam	3
໔	ສີ່	sii	4
໕	ຫ້າ	hàa	5
໖	ຫົກ	hǒk	6
໗	ເຈັດ	jět	7
໘	ແປດ	bpὲɛt	8
໙	ເກົ້າ	gâo	9

Appendix III

Test and Writing Exercise Answers

Test Answers

Test1

Matching (Page 26)

1. e   2. j   3. b   4. c   5. g
6. l   7. k   8. h   9. a   10. i

Translation (Page 26)

1. How are you?
2. (Do you) understand?
3. Is this a newspaper?
4. What's your name?
5. Is this a map or a pencil?

Test 2

Matching (Page 50)

1. m   2. k   3. n   4. l   5. o
6. e   7. p   8. g   9. b   10. a
11. j   12. q   13. d   14. f   15. h

Translation (Page 51)

1. The telephone is on the chair.
2. He is Chinese, not Japanese.
3. How much is this?
4. Where is the bathroom?
5. English is very difficult.

Test 3

Matching (Page 71)

1. j   2. n   3. f   4. a   5. q
6. m   7. b   8. l   9. d   10. p
11. c   12. e   13. h   14. i   15. k

Translation (Page 72)

1. Where do you work?
2. I like blue cars.
3. Do you like Lao food or Chinese food?
4. Where is he going?
5. You can write Lao very well.

Test 4

Telling Time (Page 98)

1. 6:15 a.m. or 6:15 p.m.
2. 3:00 p.m.
3. 4:30 p.m.
4. 2:35 a.m. or 2:35 p.m.
5. Exactly 3:00 p.m.
6. 4:50 a.m. or 4:50 p.m.
7. 12:20 p.m. (noon time)
8. 1:05 p.m.
9. 8:20 a.m. or 8:20 p.m.
10. 4:00 a.m.
11. 10:00 a.m.
12. Exactly noon.
13. 8:00 p.m.
14. 8:10 a.m. or 8:10 p.m.
15. 5:00 a.m.

Translation (Page 99)

1. I will go to the temple at noon.
2. He has been reading since eleven p.m.
3. We study Lao for three hours.
4. It's now one thirty p.m.
5. I eat breakfast at eight o'clock.

Test 5

Matching

Days (Page 119)
1. c   2. e   3. f   4. h   5. a   6. d   7. b   8. g

Months (Page 120)
1. i   2. e   3. l   4. a   5. g   6. h
7. j   8. c   9. f   10. k   11. d   12. b

Test 6

Matching (Page 137)

1. o   2. a   3. h   4. i   5. l
6. p   7. n   8. b   9. e   10. k
11. q   12. d   13. c   14. m   15. g

Translation (Page 138)

1. Now I'm going to the airport.
2. Normally, Mr. Kampan goes to work by train.
3. We want to have a Lao restaurant in America.
4. He has been in Thailand since June.
5. I don't like to listen to music.

Test 7

Matching (Page 156)

1. m   2. h   3. d   4. p   5. j
6. n   7. a   8. o   9. k   10. f
11. c   12. q   13. e   14. b   15. i

Translation (Page 157)

1. Whose notebook is on the table?
2. I can't swim.

3. I didn't swim.
4. He really misses Lao.
5. I think that western food is not very delicious.

Test 8

Matching (Page 174)

1. d   2. m   3. i   4. h   5. e
6. p   7. c   8. a   9. g   10. n
11. k   12. b   13. l   14. j   15. f

Translation (Page 175)

1. How many times a day do you brush your teeth?
    Twice a day.
2. He has a bad headache. He can't come to work.
3. I wash my hair everyday.
4. Somchai has dimples.
5. You have no brain.

Test 9

Matching (Page 192)
A.
1. c   2. e   3. d   4. k   5. m
6. l   7. h   8. f   9. b   10. j
B.
1. h   2. j   3. c   4. l   5. g
6. e   7. d   8. f   9. b   10. a
C.
1. k   2. f   3. l   4. b   5. j
6. e   7. i   8. h   9. m   10. g

Translation (Page 193)

1. What kind of work does your younger brother do?
2. He is married to a Japanese.
3. Why don't you like Lao food? Because it's very hot.
4. If I don't have money, I cannot return to Laos.
5. I think that he already has a family.

Test 10
Matching (Page 219)
A.

1. c	2. l	3. i	4. e	5. k
6. a	7. b	8. f	9. h	10. g

B.

1. k	2. h	3. e	4. d	5. c
6. m	7. a	8. j	9. f	10. g

C.

1. g	2. d	3. j	4. h	5. a
6. l	7. e	8. b	9. k	10. f

Translation (Page 221)

1. Which mango is the most delicious?
   I think that this one is the most delicious.
2. How many floors are there at your house?
   There are three.
3. When will the first ship come?
   It will come tomorrow.
4. Yesterday I bought a new watch.
5. There are five elephants at the zoo.

Writing Exercise Answer

Writing Exercise 1 (Page 38)

1. ຄາ	2. ໂກ້	3. ໄມ້, ໃມ້	4. ຕູ່
5. ເອົາ	6. ໄປ່	7. ເກົ່າ	8. ຈີ້
9. ໄຮ້, ໃຮ້	10. ເບ	11. ໄຈ, ໃຈ	12. ເຕົ່າ
13. ໂອ	14. ໄປ	15. ກຸ້	16. ໄປ່
17. ຈ່າ	18. ເຄາ	19. ກໍ່	20. ອ້າ

Writing Exercise 2 (Page 60)

1. ບາ	2. ແກະ	3. ເບືອ	4. ຕຸ
5. ບໍ	6. ເຈ	7. ກໍ	8. ເຈຽະ
9. ອໍ	10. ຈິວ	11. ເກືອ	12. ຕໍ
13. ອີ	14. ປະ	15. ກໍ	16. ເຕາະ
17. ເອີ	18. ໂກະ	19. ກົວ	20. ເກຍ, ເກັຍ, ເກັຽ

Writing Exercise 3 (Page 84)

1. ຈັນ	2. ເບີດ	3. ບັງ	4. ກວນ
5. ຈິດ	6. ເຕັມ	7. ພິນ	8. ຄັງ
9. ເກັບ	10. ຕົກ	11. ຄິນ	12. ເອັນ
13. ແຄັນ	14. ຈິງ	15. ບວນ	16. ອິງ
17. ເຄັນ	18. ເຈັບ	19. ປວດ	20. ບວກ
21. ກັນ	22. ຈິມ	23. ບັງ	24. ຊູດ
25. ກຸງ	26. ຈານ	27. ເກົ່າ	28. ຕິມ
29. ຄານ	30. ໂອກ	31. ຕຸມ	32. ບິບ

33. ກັ້ງ   34. ນັກ   35. ບ່າຍ   36. ໂອ່ງ

37. ຈ່າ   38. ເຈັບ   38. ແກບ   40. ຈ້າວ

Writing Exercise 4 (Page 106)

1. ສາ   2. ຜະ   3. ສາກ   4. ຊຸດ

5. ສຽວ   6. ຜີ   7. ແທກ   8. ທຸບ

9. ກຸງ   10. ຜິ້ງ   11. ຝັນ   12. ທາບ

13. ຝາດ   14. ຟູ່ງ

Writing Exercise 5 (Page 122)

1. ສ່ອຍ   2. ຜີ້ງ   3. ທ້ວມ   4. ອິມ

5. ຝັ່ມ   6. ຖ່ອຍ   7. ສ່ງ   8. ຊຸດ

9. ເຜີຍ   10. ຖາມ   11. ສວຍ   12. ຝັ່ງ

13. ຖ່   14. ຜ່ານ   15. ອາຍ   16. ເອົ້າ

17. ທ້ອງ   18. ຝ້າຍ   19. ສາບ   20. ເສັນ

Writing Exercise 6 (Page 144)

1. ພາ   2. ໄຂ   3. ຣຳ   4. ມູ

5. ເຂຍ   6. ເລຍ   7. ເຂີຍ   8. ທົວ

9. ເຣືອ   10. ເຟົາ   11. ທີ   12. ບໍ

13. ຝູ   14. ເທ   15. ຄຳ   16. ຄື

17. ງາ   18. ແພ   19. ຍຳ   20. ເລຍ

Writing Exercise 7 (Page 163)

1. ມ່ວງ   2. ມິກ   3. ຄຳ   4. ຍຸງ

5. ຟິມ   6. ນິ້ວ   7. ມິດ   8. ຂອງ

9. ຟັງ   10. ແຄວ   11. ຂາມ   12. ຮຮບ

13. ພູມ   14. ຣ້າມ   15. ຣາບ   16. ວ່າງ

17. ເບິ້ອງ   18. ແຂງ   19. ຄິກ   20. ແພ້ອ

Writing Exercise 8 (Page 178)

1. ຫມີ້   2. ໄຫມ, ໃຫມ

3. ໃຫຍ່, ໄຫຍ່   4. ຫມີ້

5. ຫມັ້ນ   6. ຫລາ

7. ຫວູ   8. ໂຫລ່ງ

9. ຫວັ້ນ   10. ຫວາ

About the Authors

BUASAWAN SIMMALA (ບົວສະຫວັນ ສິມມາລາ)

Buasawan Simmala was born and grew up in Vientiane, the capital of Laos. She received a Fulbright Scholarship to continue her studies in the United States and subsequently received her Master's Degree in International Commerce and Policy from George Mason University in Virginia. She is currently working on her Ph.D. in urban education from the University of Wisconsin-Milwaukee. Buasawan also works part-time as a Lao language editor, interpreter and translator. She has many private students and has taught Lao to foreigners from all over the world at the Southeast Asian Studies Summer Institute. Buasawan is proficient in Lao, Thai and Vietnamese languages.

BENJAWAN POOMSAN BECKER (ເບັນຈະວັນ ພູມແຮສນ ເບັກເກີຣ໌)

Benjawan Poomsan Becker was born in Bangkok and spent her childhood in Yasothon, a small province in Northeast Thailand. Her family is ethnic Laotian, so she grew up speaking both Thai and Lao. She graduated from Khon Kaen University in Thailand in 1990, with a B.A. in English. Benjawan gained extensive experience teaching while studying for her M.A. in Japan with Berlitz Language Schools, and in the US with Thai temples, Stanford University and private students. Now she resides in the San Francisco Bay Area where she continues to write books on the Thai and Lao languages. Benjawan is a professional interpreter and translator in both languages. Her other Lao book is "Lao-English English-Lao Dictionary for Non-Lao Speakers."

Titles from Paiboon Publishing

Title: Thai for Beginners
Author: Benjawan Poomsan Becker ©1995
Description: Designed for either self-study or classroom use. Teaches all four language skills- speaking, listening (when used in conjunction with the cassette tapes), reading and writing. Offers clear, easy, step-by-step instruction building on what has been previously learned. Used by many Thai temples and institutes in America and Thailand. Cassettes & CD available. Paperback. 270 pages. 6" x 8.5"
Book   US$12.95   Stock # 1001B
Two CDs   US$20.00   Stock # 1001CD

Title: Thai for Travelers (Pocket Book Version)
Author: Benjawan Poomsan Becker ©2006
Description: The best Thai phrase book you can find. It contains thousands of useful words and phrases for travelers in many situations. The phrases are practical and up-to-date and can be used instantly. The CD that accompanies the book will help you improve your pronunciation and expedite your Thai language learning. You will be able to speak Thai in no time! Full version on mobile phones and PocketPC also available at www.vervata.com.
Book & CD   US$15.00   Stock # 1022BCD

Title: Thai for Intermediate Learners
Author: Benjawan Poomsan Becker ©1998
Description: The continuation of Thai for Beginners Users are expected to be able to read basic Thai language. There is transliteration when new words are introduced. Teaches reading, writing and speaking at a higher level. Keeps students interested with cultural facts about Thailand. Helps expand your Thai vocabulary in a systematic way. Paperback. 220 pages. 6" x 8.5"
Book   US$12.95   Stock # 1002B
Two CDs   US$15.00   Stock # 1002CD

Title: Thai for Advanced Readers
Author: Benjawan Poomsan Becker ©2000
Description: A book that helps students practice reading Thai at an advanced level. It contains reading exercises, short essays, newspaper articles, cultural and historical facts about Thailand and miscellaneous information about the Thai language. Students need to be able to read basic Thai. Paperback. 210 pages. 6" x 8.5"
Book   US$12.95   Stock # 1003B
Two CDs   US$15.00   Stock # 1003CD

Title: Thai-English, English-Thai Dictionary for Non-Thai Speakers
Author: Benjawan Poomsan Becker ©2002
Description: Designed to help English speakers communicate in Thai. It is equally useful for
those who can read the Thai alphabet and those who can't. Most Thai-English dictionaries
either use Thai script exclusively for the Thai entries (making them difficult for westerners
to use) or use only phonetic transliteration (making it impossible to look up a word in Thai
script). This dictionary solves these problems. You will find most of the vocabulary you
are likely to need in everyday life, including basic, cultural, political and scientific terms.
Paperback. 658 pages. 4.1" x 5.6"
Book   US$15.00   Stock # 1008B

Title: Improving Your Thai Pronunciation
Author: Benjawan Poomsan Becker ©2003
Description: Designed to help foreigners maximize their potential in pronouncing Thai
words and enhance their Thai listening and speaking skills. Students will find that they have
more confidence in speaking the language and can make themselves understood better.
The book and the CDs are made to be used in combination. The course is straight forward,
easy to follow and compact. Paperback. 48 pages. 5" x 7.5" + One-hour CD
Book & CD   US$15.00   Stock # 1011BCD

Title: Thai for Lovers
Author: Nit & Jack Ajee ©1999
Description: An ideal book for lovers. A short cut to romantic communication in Thailand.
There are useful sentences with their Thai translations throughout the book. You won't
find any Thai language book more fun and user-friendly.
Rated R! Paperback. 190 pages. 6" x 8.5"
Book   US$13.95   Stock #: 1004B
Two CDs   US$17.00   Stock #: 1004CD

Title: Thai for Gay Tourists
Author: Saksit Pakdeesiam ©2001
Description: The ultimate language guide for gay and bisexual men visiting Thailand. Lots
of gay oriented language, culture, commentaries and other information. Instant sentences
for convenient use by gay visitors. Fun and sexy. The best way to communicate with your
Thai gay friends and partners! Rated R! Paperback. 220 pages. 6" x 8.5"
Book   US$13.95   Stock # 1007B
Two Tape Set   US$17.00   Stock # 1007T

Title: Thailand Fever
Authors: Chris Pirazzi and Vitida Vasant ©2005
Description: A road map for Thai-Western relationships. The must-have relationship guide-
book which lets each of you finally express complex issues of both cultures. Thailand Fever
is an astonishing, one-of-a-kind, bilingual expose of the cultural secrets that are the key
to a smooth Thai-Western relationship. Paperback. 258 pages. 6" x 8.5"
Book   US$15.95   Stock # 1017B

Title: Thai-English, English-Thai Software Dictionary
for Palm OS PDAs With Search-by-Sound
Authors: Benjawan Poomsan Becker and Chris Pirazzi ©2003
Description: This software dictionary provides instant access to 21,000 English, Phonetic
and Thai Palm OS PDA with large, clear fonts and everyday vocabulary. If you're not familiar
with the Thai alphabet, you can also look up Thai words by their sounds. Perfect for the

casual traveller or the dedicated Thai learner. Must have a Palm OS PDA and access to the Internet in order to use this product.
Book & CD-ROM   US$39.95   Stock # 1013BCD-ROM

Title: Thai for Beginners Software
Authors: Benjawan Poomsan Becker and Dominique Mayrand ©2004
Description: Best Thai language software available in the market! Designed especially for non-romanized written Thai to help you to rapidly improve your listening and reading skills! Over 3,000 recordings of both male and female voices. The content is similar to the book Thai for Beginners, but with interactive exercises and much more instantly useful words and phrases. Multiple easy-to-read font styles and sizes. Super-crisp enhanced text with romanized transliteration which can be turned on or off for all items.
Book & CD-ROM   US$40.00   Stock # 1016BCD-ROM

Title: Lao-English, English-Lao Dictionary for Non-Lao Speakers
Authors: Benjawan Poomsan Becker & Khamphan Mingbuapha ©2003
Description: Designed to help English speakers communicate in Lao. This practical dictionary is useful both in Laos and in Northeast Thailand. Students can use it without having to learn the Lao alphabet. However, there is a comprehensive introduction to the Lao writing system and pronunciation. The transliteration system is the same as that used in Paiboon Publishing's other books. It contains most of the vocabulary used in everyday life, including basic, cultural, political and scientific terms. Paperback. 780 pages. 4.1" x 5.6"
Book   US$15.00   Stock # 1010B

Title: Lao for Beginners
Authors: Buasawan Simmala and Benjawan Poomsan Becker ©2003
Description: Designed for either self-study or classroom use. Teaches all four language skills- speaking, listening (when used in conjunction with the audio), reading and writing. Offers clear, easy, step-by-step instruction building on what has been previously learned. Paperback. 292 pages. 6" x 8.5"
Book   US$12.95   Stock # 1012B
Three CDs   US$20.00   Stock # 1012CD

Title: Cambodian for Beginners
Author: Richard K. Gilbert ©2008
Description: Designed for either self-study or classroom use. Teaches all four language skills- speaking, listening (when used in conjunction with the CDs), reading and writing. Offers clear, easy, step-by-step instruction building on what has been previously learned. Paperback. 290 pages. 6" x 8.5"
Book   US$15.00   Stock # 1015B
Three CDs   US$20.00   Stock # 1015CD

Title: Burmese for Beginners
Author: Gene Mesher ©2006
Description: Designed for either self-study or classroom use. Teaches all four language skills- speaking, listening (when used in conjunction with the CDs), reading and writing. Offers clear, easy, step-by-step instruction building on what has been previously learned. Paperback. 320 pages. 6" x 8.5"
Book   US$12.95   Stock # 1019B
Three CDs   US$20.00   Stock # 1019CD

Title: Vietnamese for Beginners
Author: Jake Catlett ©2008
Description: Designed for either self-study or classroom use. Teaches all four language skills- speaking, listening (when used in conjunction with the CDs), reading and writing. Offers clear, easy, step-by-step instruction building on what has been previously learned. Paperback. 292 pages. 6" x 8.5"
Book   US$15.00   Stock # 1020B
Three CDs   US$20.00   Stock # 1020CD

Title: Tai Go No Kiso
Author: Benjawan Poomsan Becker ©2002
Description: Thai for Japanese speakers. Japanese version of Thai for Beginners. Paperback. 262 pages. 6" x 8.5"
Book   US$12.95   Stock # 1009B
Three Tape Set   US$20.00   Stock # 1009T

Title: Thai fuer Anfaenger
Author: Benjawan Poomsan Becker ©2000
Description: Thai for German speakers. German version of Thai for Beginners. Paperback. 245 pages. 6" x 8.5"
Book   US$13.95   Stock # 1005B
Two CDs   US$20.00   Stock # 1005CD

Title: Practical Thai Conversation DVD Volume 1
Author: Benjawan Poomsan Becker ©2005
Description: This new media for learning Thai comes with a booklet and a DVD. You will enjoy watching and listening to this program and learn the Thai language in a way you have never done before. Use it on your TV, desktop or laptop. The course is straight forward, easy to follow and compact. A must-have for all Thai learners! DVD and Paperback, 65 pages 4.8" x 7.1"
Book & DVD   US$15.00   Stock # 1018BDVD

Title: Practical Thai Conversation DVD Volume 2
Author: Benjawan Poomsan Becker ©2006
Description: Designed for intermediate Thai learners! This new media for learning Thai comes with a booklet and a DVD. You will enjoy watching and listening to this program and learn the Thai language in a way you have never done before. Use it on your TV, desktop or laptop. The course is straight forward, easy to follow and compact. DVD and Paperback, 60 pages 4.8" x 7.1"
Book & DVD   US$15.00   Stock # 1021BDVD

Title: Thai Touch
Author: Richard Rubacher ©2006
Description: The good and the bad of the Land of Smiles are told with a comic touch. The book focuses on the spiritual and mystical side of the magical kingdom as well as its dark side. The good and the bad are told with a comic touch. The Sex Baron, the Naughty & Nice Massage Parlors, the "Bangkok haircut" and Bar Girls & the Pendulum are contrasted with tales of the Thai Forrest Gump, the Spiritual Banker of Thailand and the 72-year old woman whose breasts spout miracle milk. Paperback. 220 pages. 5" x 7.5"
Book   US$19.95   Stock #1024B

Title: How to Buy Land and Build a House in Thailand
Author: Philip Bryce ©2006
Description: This book contains essential information for anyone contemplating buying or leasing land and building a house in Thailand. Subjects covered: land ownership options, land titles, taxes, permits, lawyers, architects and builders. Also includes English/Thai building words and phrases and common Thai building techniques. Learn how to build your dream house in Thailand that is well made, structurally sound and nicely finished. Paperback. 6" x 8.5"
Book   US$19.95   Stock #1025B

Title: Retiring in Thailand
Authors: Philip Bryce and Sunisa Wongdee Terlecky ©2007
Description: A very useful guide for those who are interested in retiring in Thailand. It contains critical information for retirees, such as how to get a retirement visa, banking, health care, renting and buying property, everyday life issues and other important retirement factors. It also lists Thailand's top retirement locations. It's a must for anyone considering living the good life in the Land of Smiles. 6" x 8.5"
Book   US$19.95   Stock #1026B

Title: How to Establish a Successful Business in Thailand
Author: Philip Wylie ©2007
Description: This is the perfect book for anyone thinking of starting or buying a business in Thailand. This book will save readers lots of headaches, time and money. This guide is full of information on how to run a business in Thailand including practical tips by successful foreign business people from different trades, such as guest house, bar trade, e-commerce, export and restaurant. This is an essential guide for all foreigners thinking of doing business - or improving their business - in Thailand.
Book   US$19.95   Stock #1031B

Title: Speak Like A Thai Volume 1
-Contemporary Thai Expressions-
Author: Benjawan Poomsan Becker ©2007
Description: This series of books and CDs is a collection of numerous words and expressions used by modern Thai speakers. It will help you to understand colloquial Thai and to express yourself naturally. You will not find these phases in most textbooks. It's a language course that all Thai learners have been waiting for. Impress your Thai friends with the real spoken Thai. Lots of fun. Good for students of all levels.
Book & CD   US$15.00   Stock # 1028BCD

Title: Speak Like A Thai Volume 2
-Thai Slang and Idioms-
Author: Benjawan Poomsan Becker ©2007
Description: This volume continues the fun of learning the real Thai language. It can be used independently. However, you should be comfortable speaking the Thai phrases from the first volume before you use this one. You will not find these words and phases in any textbooks. It's a language course that all Thai learners have been waiting for. Impress your Thai friends even more. Lots of fun. Good for students of all levels.
Book & CD   US$15.00   Stock # 1029BCD

Title: Speak Like A Thai Volume 3
-Thai Proverbs and Sayings-
Author: Benjawan Poomsan Becker ©2007
Description: The third volume is an excellent supplementary resource for all Thai learners. Common Thai proverbs and sayings listed in the book with the literal translations will help you understand Thai ways of thinking that are differnt from yours. You can listen to these proverbs and sayings over and over on the CD. Sprinkle them here and there in your conversation. Your Thai friend will be surprised and appreciate your insight into Thai culture. Good for intermdiate and advanced students, but beginners can use it for reference.
Book & CD   US$15.00   Stock # 1030BCD

Title: Speak Like a Thai Volume 4
-Heart Words-
Author: Benjawan Poomsan Becker ©2008
Description: "Heart" Words contains 300 common contemporary "heart" words and phrases. They are recorded on the CD and explained in the booklet with a brief translation, a literal translation and used in a sample phrase or sentence. More than a hundred bonus "heart" words are included in the booklet for your reference. Listen and learn how Thai people express their feelings and thoughts. You will gain significant insight about the Thai people and their social contexts.
Book & CD   US$15.00   Stock # 1033BCD

Title: Speak Like a Thai Volume 5
-Northeastern Dialect-
Author: Benjawan Poomsan Becker ©2008
Description: Northeastern Dialect contains 500 Isaan words and phrases which have been carefully chosen from real life situations. They are recorded on the CD and explained in the booklet with a brief translation and a literal translation when needed. Throughout the book there are also lists of many Isaan words that are different from standard Thai. This is a fun program that will bring a smile to the face of your Isaan friends.
Book & CD   US$15.00   Stock # 1034BCD

Title: Speak like a Thai Volume 6
-Real Life Conversations-
Author: Benjawan Poomsan Becker ©2009
Description:A great resource for both beginners and more advanced students! This program will help you feel more comfortable speaking Thai and you will sound more like a native. The idioms and expressions in this program are actually used in real life and won't be seen in regular textbooks. There are 20 conversations in this program featuring different types of situations.

The audio CD accompanying this booklet contains all these dialogs. Each conversation is first recorded at normal speed in Thai - just like you would hear it in real life. The conversation is then presented with the English translation first and then the Thai with some time for you to repeat.

Some of the conversations are also contained in video format on a separate DVD product. You can watch and learn them from our Practical Thai Conversations DVD Volume 1 and Volume 2.

Listen to this program over and over and practice and practice. You will be able to Speak Like A Thai in no time. *ALL SPEAK LIKE A THAI VOLUMES CAN BE USED INDEPENDENTLY*
Book & CD   US$15.00   Stock # 1038BCD

Title: Thai Law for Foreigners
Author: Ruengsak Thongkaew and Benjawan Poomsan ©2008
Description: Thai law made easy for foreigners. This unique book includes information regarding immigration, family, property, civil and criminal law used in Thailand. Very useful for both visitors and those who live in Thailand. Written by an experienced Thai trial lawyer. It contains both the Thai text and full English translation.
Book $21.95   Stock # 1032B

Title: New Three-Way Thai-English, English-Thai Pocket Dictionary for English Speakers with Tones and Classifiers
Authors: Benjawan Poomsan Becker and Chris Pirazzi ©2009
Description: This practical Thai English, English Thai dictionary is designed to help English speakers communicate in Thai, whether or not you can read the Thai alphabet. All Thai words are listed in both Thai script and an easy-to-learn, English-like pronunciation system that fully expresses the Thai sound, including the tones and everything else you need to speak and understand Thai words correctly. It's a perfect fit with our other books, such as Thai for Beginners.

Unlike traditional dictionaries, there are three sections: you can look up an English word in the English section, look up a Thai word you read using the Thai Script section, or look up a Thai word you hear by its sound in the unique Thai Sound section.

What's New:
• More words: 28,000+ entries and 36,000+ definitions
• Classifiers now listed for more than 15,000 noun entries
• Thorough editing and corrections done on existing entries
• Full pronunciation provided for all Thai words, including syllable stress
• Added crucial usage information (object position) for transitive verbs
• Totally updated with many new, modern terms
• Larger fonts: easy on the eye

Whether you are visiting Thailand for a short while or living there permanently, in this dictionary you will find most of the vocabulary used in everyday life, including basic medical, cultural, political and scientific terms.

It's the one dictionary you can really use! And it comes in a portable size that is easy to carry around Thailand. Paperback: 982 pages
Book: US$18.00   Stock # 1037B